About the Author

From inauspicious beginnings in a small town in Tennessee, Fred Thompson has had one of the most unusual and interesting careers on the American scene today. It has encompassed the law, politics, radio, television, and motion pictures.

Thompson served eight years as a Senator from Tennessee, and in 2008 sought the Republican nomination for President of the United States. First elected to the United States Senate in 1994, he was returned to office by the people of Tennessee two years later with more votes than any candidate for any office in the state's history at that time. He served as Chairman of the Senate Governmental Affairs Committee, and as a member of the Finance Committee as well as the Select Committee on Intelligence. In 2002, Senator Thompson walked away from an easy reelection victory to seek new challenges.

Prior to his election, Thompson maintained law offices in Nashville and Washington. Earlier in his career, he served as an Assistant U.S. Attorney in Tennessee. In 1973, he was appointed by Senator Howard Baker to serve as Minority Counsel to the Senate Watergate Committee, where Thompson first gained national attention for leading the line of inquiry that revealed the audiotaping system in the White

House Oval Office. He detailed his Watergate experience in his Watergate memoir, *At That Point in Time.*

Senator Thompson first appeared on-screen in the film *Marie* in 1985, portraying himself in the fact-based story of a high-profile public corruption case he handled in Tennessee. Since then, he has appeared in numerous movies, including *No Way Out, In the Line of Fire, Die Hard II, Days of Thunder,* and *The Hunt for Red October,* and will appear in Disney's *Secretariat,* set for release in October, 2010. Recently, he became known for his portrayal of New York District Attorney Arthur Branch on the Emmy Award–winning NBC television drama *Law & Order.*

In 2005, Senator Thompson was named by President Bush as an advisor to Supreme Court Chief Justice nominee John Roberts, helping to move his nomination through the Senate confirmation process. Thompson continued his public service as Chairman of the State Department's International Security Advisory Board.

He currently hosts *The Fred Thompson Show,* a nationally syndicated radio talk show. He resides in McLean, Virginia, with his wife, Jeri, daughter, Hayden, and son, Sammy.

Also by Fred Thompson

At That Point in Time:
The Inside Story of the Senate
Watergate Committee

Teaching the Pig to Dance

A MEMOIR

Fred Thompson

CROWN
FORUM
NEW YORK

Published in the United States by Crown Forum, an imprint of the
Crown Publishing Group, a division of Random House, Inc., New York.

www.crownpublishing.com

CROWN FORUM with colophon is a registered trademark of
Random House, Inc.

Library of Congress Cataloging-in-Publication Data
Thompson, Fred.
Teaching the pig to dance: a memoir / Fred Thompson.—1st ed.
1. Thompson, Fred, 1942 Aug. 19– 2. Legislators—U.S.—Biography.
3. U.S. Congress. Senate—Biography. 4. Presidentional candidates—
U.S.—Biography. 5. Lawyers—Tennessee—Biography. 6. Actors—U.S.—
Biography. 7. Lawrenceburg (Tenn.)—Biography. I. Title.
E840.8.T475A3 2010
328.73'092—dc22
[B]   2009053528

ISBN 978-0-307-46028-8

PRINTED IN THE UNITED STATES OF AMERICA

Design by Ralph Fowler/rlfdesign

10   9   8   7   6   5   4   3   2   1

First Edition

In memory of my daughter, Betsy

Contents

Contents

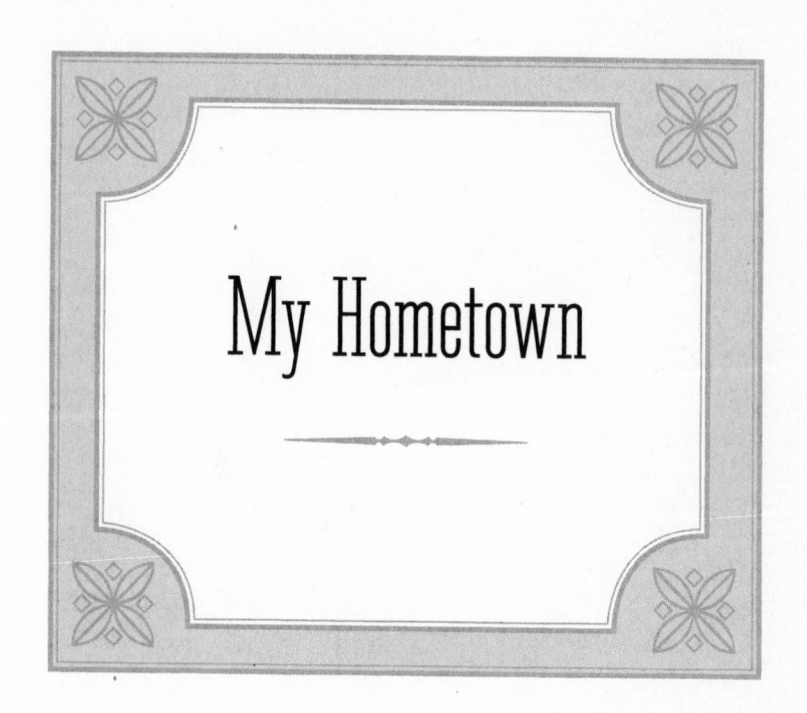

My Hometown

IN THE PART of the country where I come from, most people are proud of their hometown. Folks in Linden, Tennessee, are a good example of that. Situated in rural country in Middle Tennessee, about fifty-seven miles from where I grew up, Linden had about a thousand residents. One day during the Cuban missile crisis in 1962, the coffee drinkers at the drugstore on the town square noticed out the window that one of the local good old boys had his pickup truck loaded with what appeared to be his worldly possessions. As he walked into the drugstore to buy supplies, one of the coffee-drinking busybodies said to him:

"Lem, looks like you're moving out. What's up?"

"Ain't you boys heard about the missile crisis?" Lem replied.

The fellow answered, "Yeah, but what makes you think they're gonna bomb Linden?"

Lem said, "It's the county seat, ain't it?"

· · ·

Well, Lawrenceburg is a county seat, too. This meant that Lawrenceburg had a courthouse with a square. Every courthouse in the state was located to be not more than a half day's horse ride from any part of the county. It also meant that Lawrenceburg was the location of the county fair. As the center of county culture, it had a movie theater. And it had an organized Little League. In short, growing up in the county seat was pretty much a privileged situation.

Like thousands of little towns across America, it was populated mostly by folks who had grown up on the farm and come to town to enjoy the fruits of a better life. Usually having little in the way of a formal education, a man's reputation for hard work and keeping his word were his most valuable assets. That's the way it was with my people and just about everybody they knew. It's not that our town didn't have its share of scalawags. As one old-timer put it, "We weren't big enough to have a town drunk, so a few of us had to take turns."

What we did have for sure was more than our share of characters, used-car lots, and churches, all of which were an important part of my years growing up.

Some time ago I decided to write my story—a story that began in Lawrenceburg. You know, the obligatory autobiography, written by anyone with the necessary fifteen minutes of fame or success. It would be about how I left Lawrenceburg and, over the years, had some very interesting adventures. There were the early days when I was a federal prosecutor. Then there would be a part about my role as counsel for the Watergate committee, and my part in revealing the taping system in the Nixon White House. Then, of course, I would relate some of my experiences in the movie business as well as on the TV show *Law & Order*. And there would be the eight years I spent in the U.S. Senate (which made me long for the realism and sincerity of Hollywood). Naturally, I would also talk about my presidential campaign (described by one of my comedian friends as probably the most stressful three weeks of my life).

Finally, there would be the concluding chapter that we are all too familiar with, wherein I would give my instructions to a waiting America as to what must be done to meet the "challenges of our time." It's amazing how brilliant and insightful a fellow becomes when he leaves elective office and can't do a thing about all those problems.

I even had a title for that book picked out: *Why I've Had Such a Hard Time Keeping a Job.*

In all seriousness, that book I had in mind was going to be more than just old, warmed-over "war stories." I was going to write about opportunities presenting themselves and why I took some and not others. There's a lot to be said for seizing the moment, and I thought a book about the remarkable interconnectedness of the experiences I've had—how a decision I made has so often seemed to lead inexorably to consequences and opportunities that I never foresaw—might be somewhat instructive.

Well, this is not that book. As I got into the process, I discovered that what I was writing about was what happened *before* I left Lawrenceburg, not after I left. The thought of those times didn't necessarily make me nostalgic, but they did make me feel good. I was revisiting and laughing with some of the most interesting characters and funniest people you'd ever hope to meet, not the least of whom was my own dad.

The fact is that the people I knew and the experiences I had in that little town formed the prism through which I have viewed the world, and they shaped the way I have dealt with events throughout my life. Those growing-up years in Lawrenceburg left me with a particular take on life. A saying I often heard sort of typifies it. Usually said with a smile, it is "Ain't nobody gonna get out of this old world alive anyway, son," often said to put things into perspective when times were getting rough.

And, perhaps not surprisingly, I heard sayings like that more than a couple of times from more than a few people. From the girl I married as a teenager and her family, to the teachers, coaches, preachers, and most of all my mom and dad, they encouraged and tolerated this young ne'er-do-well kid with no apparent prospects. They cajoled me, inspired me, and shepherded me from childhood to manhood. It was not an easy trip for any of us, but by the time I left Lawrenceburg, I had learned some valuable lessons and had the confidence to take on the world. (Of course, the world had the confidence to take on me, too, but that's another story.)

There's another old saying that comes to mind: "Life is a comedy for those who think and a tragedy for those who feel." I can add to that. Where I come from, tragedy and comedy were often served at the same table. But the lessons that grew out of those experiences were grounded in the kind of commonsense view of life and living that today is, unfortunately, all too uncommon.

So I decided to write about what I wanted to write about. Stories about growing up—in every sense of the word. Stories about Lawrenceburg. It's about time Lawrenceburg had the recognition. After all, it *is* the county seat.

The Tree the Acorn
Fell From

I SUPPOSE everyone remembers where they were when they realized they were not going to be the leader of the free world. I know I do. It was on January 19, 2008, in the back of a bus rolling down a road just outside of Charleston, South Carolina, when early exit-poll results started coming in from the South Carolina presidential primary. I had edged out McCain in Iowa and come in ahead of Romney and Giuliani in South Carolina. The bad news is I came in third in both places. Not good enough. In presidential primary politics, many are called but few are chosen. I wasn't, and it was time to hang it up.

I had walked through many doors of opportunity in my life and was used to finding something good on the other side. In fact, for me the 2008 primary season was officially the first time in my life I had proven (in a most public way) that I couldn't accomplish something I had set out to do. It was a rather humbling experience. It occurred to me that, to paraphrase one of Churchill's comments, perhaps I had more to be humble about than I had realized. It also occurred to me that this was a pretty doggone expensive way to achieve a little humility. Maybe I needed to be reminded of what an old-timer told me years ago after I'd had some success: "Just remember, son, the turnout at your funeral is still going to depend a hell of a lot on the weather."

Yeah, yeah, I accepted all that, but for some reason the immortal words of Dick Tuck seemed more appropriate. Tuck was a Democratic operative famous before and during Watergate as a political prankster. When President Nixon adopted the campaign slogan "Nixon's the One," Tuck had several women boisterously show up at a Nixon rally in pregnancy costumes, waving signs saying "Nixon's the One."

Tuck finally ran for office himself—for the state senate in California. On Election Night, when it became obvious he was receiving a drubbing, he went before his supporters and the media and said, "The people have spoken . . . the bastards."

By the morning of January 20, I had other things to be thinking about. By then, I was at the bedside of my mother at Vanderbilt Hospital in Nashville. At eighty-seven, she was enduring her latest and most severe bout of pneumonia, compounded by several other ailments. She did not look good at all. In fact, the doctor and the head nurse privately talked to me in very somber tones, uttering "We've done all that we can do"–type comments. Of course, they didn't take into account the fact that "Mrs. Ruth" was tough as a pine knot. She hated hospitals with an extraordinary passion and was totally exhausted from the constant visits by hospital personnel. For the next twenty-four hours, I camped outside her room in a chair and made the medical staff justify their admission before I would let them in. She got some rest and soon was improving, just as she had many times before. She and I have concluded that most people who die in hospitals flatline from aggravation and lack of sleep.

Literally, almost overnight, I had gone from the most public, intrusive, self-centered existence known to man to the exact opposite—the quiet of my mother's room late at night. It was a quick journey from manufactured reality to reality. I smiled as I remembered her telling me when I was a kid: "Freddie, you can be anything you want to be, but please just don't be a lawyer or a politician." Over the years I think she changed her mind about my becoming a lawyer, but I don't think she ever quite fully bought into the politician part. I knew that she'd laugh when I told her, "If it's any consolation, I didn't turn out to be much of a politician after all."

My career choices were not entirely my fault. The atmosphere I grew up in in Lawrenceburg, Tennessee, was dense with politics and debates, the exploits of public figures and larger-than-life characters engaged in bare-knuckled political theater. I merely inhaled.

I am willing to bet that the town square in Lawrenceburg

has never been compared to Times Square in New York. But they say that if you stand in Times Square long enough, everybody you know will pass by. By the same token, when I think about the square in Lawrenceburg, it occurs to me that every major development in my life can be traced back to there.

In the 1950s, Lawrenceburg was a little town of six or seven thousand. It is seventy-two miles south of Nashville and just north of the Alabama state line. My folks grew up on farms in Lawrence County and came to town to start their new life together, as so many of the country kids did. By the time I came along, the town square, just like the people, had shed some of its rougher edges, although an ample number of pool halls still served as the town's designated dens of iniquity.

The courthouse had a yard around it often populated by a good number of tobacco-chewing checker players. Between games they swapped knives and lies and talked politics. The square had mostly old two- and three-story buildings housing dry goods, hardware, and drugstores as well as "the bank." The square was the center of commerce for the county, and the center of the universe, as far as I was concerned. A fellow could cash his check, shoot a game of pool, buy his tags, grab a burger, and pick up a new shirt for Saturday night without ever having to get in his car.

Today, I can stand in that square and in my mind's eye envision the sight of the old Princess Theater, where I saw my first movie. The "new" Crockett Theater, built when I was in grade school, was where I spent as much time as possible as a boy. It also was the town's main date destination. I can also see the locations of two different little cafés my grandparents owned and ran. Farther around the square are the hall where I shot my first pool and the spot where I sold my first newspaper. I also see the site of my first law office and where I made my announcement speech when I first ran for the Senate. I'm not sure how many folks were there for that, but there were thousands the night we had a rally during my presidential campaign. The courthouse was where I heard numerous political speeches, tried my first lawsuit, and saw my first election returns.

On election night, they would set up a big blackboard in the yard outside the courthouse and keep a running tally as the precinct boxes came in—if they came in. Boxes being stolen and thrown into the river or hidden in the woods was not unheard of on election night, and neither was gunplay—even in the courthouse. For a time, it was easier to steal an election than it was to buy a beer in Lawrence County.

The old courthouse was built in 1905, a Gothic—or perhaps pre-Gothic—structure, and when I started practicing law, cases were still being tried in the large second-floor courtroom where lawyers had to plead their cases while dodging the tobacco cans strategically placed around the room to catch the water when it rained.

This whole tableau was presided over by Davy Crockett.

Actually, it was Davy Crockett's full-length statue on the south side of the square. Davy had "laid out" the town of Lawrenceburg as a surveyor, lived there, and run a mill for a period of time. But Davy was a traveling man and therefore was claimed by a lot of different folks around the state and elsewhere. However, we were the only one with a Davy Crockett statue, which, in our eyes, legitimized our claim. He was, of course, a hunter, a trapper, a congressman, and a hero at the Alamo. He was also cantankerous, even bucking Andrew Jackson. And when he was defeated for Congress, he called a delegation together and told his constituents, "You all can go to hell, I am going to Texas." As it turned out, he stayed in Texas a lot longer than he intended to.

It just seemed appropriate to have old Davy permanently standing in the middle of Lawrenceburg. We liked his grit and we liked his style. Actually, we didn't pay that much attention to him until the miracle of television intervened and changed the way we perceived Davy's importance forever. I refer, of course, to the Walt Disney television series starring Fess Parker as Davy Crockett, which had half the little boys in America (and all them in the town of Lawrenceburg) wearing coonskin caps. Lawrenceburg and our statue got their share of notoriety and attention, and before the dust was settled we had Crockett Theater, a Crockett School, a Crockett Service Station, a Crockett Beauty Salon, a Crockett State Park, as well as many other namings. As it turned out, we were among the first people in the world to realize that nothing is important or noteworthy until it appears on television.

Most of us have learned that the significance of the people and places in your life is not so obvious until you are looking at them in your rearview mirror. Actually, the transitions my parents saw and made surpass any that I have experienced. And they, like millions of others, did it anonymously and without fanfare. I never heard a lot of stories about the Great Depression, but it was obvious that in many ways it defined my parents' childhood. They were farmers and sharecroppers in rural Lawrence County, but they had plenty to eat, which is all their neighbors had. On the Thompson side, that hardscrabble life produced a couple of six-foot-five-inch brothers who were well "filled out"—my grandfather, Edgar, and his brother. I never knew which of the stories I heard about Pa Thompson were true, but one of the more persistent had to do with the time a young mule kicked at him and he grabbed the mule's hind legs and ran him around the barnyard. He was a giant by the standards of the day. Ma Thompson was an Allen—rough-hewn folks like the Thompsons, except a little more entrepreneurial. Many years after most of that generation had passed away, "Uncle Percy" Allen, who was in his nineties, was asked by some of the grandchildren about the Thompsons and the Allens. Pressed, he finally said with a wry smile, "Well, the Allens made a whole lot of whiskey. And the Thompsons drank most of it." Uncle Percy may have been exhibiting the sense of humor that both clans were known for; then again, maybe not.

"Drinkin'" had a different meaning for country folks in those days. There was no such thing as a social drinker. Either you drank or you didn't, and drinking meant getting rip-roaring drunk. When a young girl would talk about meeting a new young man, a discussion would ensue in hushed tones as to whether or not he "drank." A drinker was further defined as either a "mean drunk" or a "happy drunk." I got the impression that my daddy may have been both, depending on the occasion.

All I know is that I never saw a drop of alcohol in the house of either my parents or my grandparents. Actually, it's all consistent with what I learned about my ancestors over the years and so many of their neighbors. They had a hard life but loved to laugh and joke and have a good time. And while the men were wild in their youth, they grew up, joined the church, and became domesticated when the time came.

My dad was a prime example of that. As a young man, Fletcher was the oldest of four brothers, six feet tall, slender, and tough with wavy hair. His pictures reflect the fact that he looked like John Dillinger. He hired out to plow a mule for fifty cents a day and drank and fought on Saturday nights.

During the Depression he wanted to leave and become a Golden Gloves boxer, but he was afraid his family couldn't survive without him. The only legacy that came from his fighting days was a partial gold tooth he had from an encounter with a deputy sheriff.

Dad made it through the eighth grade. In ones and twos, the Thompsons, having "enjoyed" the rustic life as much as they could stand, came to town to live. My mom, Ruth Bradley, was a country girl from a few roads over and the oldest of five children. The Bradleys were a more serious bunch. Pa Bradley's father died when he was a child. He was sixteen when he married Ma Bradley, who was eighteen. He worked the fields, the mines, and at anything else that came along. Everyone said he was the hardest worker they had ever seen. My mother adored him. Her mom also worked the fields, raised the family, and was a pretty good carpenter. She made several pieces of the furniture in their home. Young Ruth was sent to the cotton fields at an early age. In later years, when Dad would wax nostalgic about growing up on the farm and expressed a desire to someday get back to the country, Mama would have none of it. Growing up on a farm in Tennessee during the Depression had not been her idea of fun. She'd seen enough of it for a lifetime and was determined never to go back. And she didn't.

Shortly after Dad married Mom, it became obvious that Fletcher had met his match. By the time I came along, Mom had laid down the law and Dad had renounced his old habits, joined the church, and was taking a very dim view of the vices that he had almost perfected during his single days. For the rest of his life he never drank a drop, and he never missed a day's work except for illness. He walked in the door every night at 6 o'clock to sit down for a supper that was already waiting on him. I never saw my parents engage in so much as a heated argument. My mom's influence reminded me of a story about a fellow who, after years of low-down behavior, was hit across the head by a two-by-four and then reformed. "Nobody ever explained things to me like that before," he said.

One thing that didn't change about Fletch was his take on life. He seldom saw a situation that didn't call for a humorous or sardonic comment. One of my earliest childhood memories is one night after Wednesday Bible study, when I was in the backseat of the car as we were driving home. We stopped at a red light, and a pitiful, haggard old lady walked across the street in front of us. Dad said, "You know, I believe that is the ugliest human being I have ever seen in my life." Mama responded, "Why, Fletcher, she can't help it." To which Dad replied, "No, but she could stay home." His comments were often so outrageous that Mom spent a good part of her life trying to stifle laughter in front of the children, who she knew were receiving a terrible example.

There was a running joke in our family. When Mom would go to the beautician, she would tell Dad where she was going. Upon her return, she would walk into the room, and Dad would take one look at her and say, "Change your mind?" or "Beauty shop closed?" Mom would fain outrage as she would walk into the other room, smiling.

Mom loved to go antique shopping. There have always been plenty of "antique" shops to choose from in Tennessee. Granted, some of them in a Southern gesture of good humor and honesty had signs out front, for "Antiques and Junkue," but Mom would buy an old piece of furniture from time to time. She collected many pieces and more than a few sets of "Flow Blue" china from these shops. It's fair to say that Dad wasn't up on all of this.

One of her antiques is a table with twisted legs. It's called a "barley twist," named for the twisted plugs of chewing tobacco that were common years ago. One evening, Mom and Dad went to an antique auction in Columbia, Tennessee. Along with them was Mom's sister, Aunt Freda, and her husband, Robert.

Anyway, Mom and Aunt Freda were seated at the auction in one row, and Dad and Robert, who was just as big a cutup as Dad was, were seated behind them. They were all talking when the auctioneer announced the next item for sale— "Now, ladies and gentlemen, we are going to sell one with twisted legs"—as the crowd quieted down. Quick as a wink, Dad jumped up and said, loud enough for all around him to hear, "Robert, I've got to get down there! They're getting ready to sell my wife!" Thirty years later, Mom still laughs about it.

Dad not only brought home the bacon, he brought home an interesting variety of other things, too. One July day in 1954, he brought home a new Ping-Pong table. At least that's what he called it. He had a friend build it for him. It was a little high off the ground for us kids, but we painted it green, got a net and some paddles, and I became very popular in the neighborhood for a while. We kept it outside unless it was raining, at which point we would shove it into the small basement under the house.

Unfortunately, if it was a hard rain and stormy, the basement was most likely where the Thompsons would be, too. The problem was that Mom was deathly afraid of storms. Growing up in the country, as a kid she had seen some bad ones. Her family had always had what was called a "storm cellar" for such occasions, where canned and other goods were kept, and which provided a temporary refuge while the family huddled and waited to see if the house was going to be blown away. It opened flat to the ground and was deep and wide enough to shelter the whole family. All of this made a lasting impression on Mom, who years later would walk the floor, wring her hands, seek the low ground, and insist that her two overgrown sons get under the bed. We dutifully complied until we couldn't stuff ourselves under there anymore. If Dad was home he humored her, although he would have been just fine reading the paper until the crisis passed.

On one particularly rough-weather day, Mom, Dad, my younger brother Ken, and I were waiting it out in the basement, with no one but Mom coming even remotely close to thinking it was necessary for us to be down there with no TV or radio for entertainment. Mom was beside herself, saying, "What are we going to do? What are we going to do?" Dad looked over in the corner of the basement and said, "Well, I have always heard that the best thing to do at a time like this is to get under a green Ping-Pong table." I am sure that at that point, through the thunder and lightning, anyone on the street could have heard the gales of laughter coming from the male Thompsons. Dad had delivered such a perfect line that even Mom got tickled.

There are certain turning points in every family when issues are resolved or new understandings are reached. The green Ping-Pong table provided one for us. I don't recall Mom ever carrying on about a storm again. For years afterward, if the weather was looking bad, Dad, Ken, or I would say, "Okay, do we have a green Ping-Pong table?" And that would be the end of it. I never knew if Mom got over her fear or it just wasn't worth the aggravation anymore.

Dad got his irreverence honestly. His mother, Ma Thompson, was what could only be described as a "pistol." She was outgoing, everybody's friend, and holder of the world's record on funeral attendances—all while dispensing large amounts of her famous red velvet cake. She once had a "gourder," an egg-size tumor, removed from her neck. The next day, she was around town carrying it in a cloth, unwrapping it and showing it to her friends.

When I was a small boy, I called her "Ma Thompson" the way my cousin did. One day she looked at me and said, "Would it hurt you to call me Mrs. Thompson the way everybody else does?" Of course, I took her seriously and started calling her Mrs. Thompson. She thought it was the funniest thing ever. As I got older, I was always wanting to go over to her house on Saturdays because I knew that she would invariably slip me the twenty cents necessary to go to the movies. I never really knew whether or not it was an act of generosity or she just found me to be boring.

Although Ma Thompson, with her outgoing personality and ready laughter, was the center of attention everywhere she went, Pa Thompson had a wit that was as dry as a Death Valley bone, though seldom used. One of the three or four cafés they owned and operated in Lawrenceburg over the years of my youth was the Colonial Café, downtown across from the city hall. In a circumstance I've never seen before or since, right next door was a café, the Dixie Grill, that was almost identical to the Colonial. Same store front, same size, and same sort of food.

One day Pa Thompson was standing out in front of the Colonial smoking a cigarette. A stranger pulled up, got out of his car, looked at both restaurants, and asked Pa Thompson which of the restaurants he should go to. Pa Thompson told him, "Don't make any difference. Whichever one you go to, you'll wish you'd gone to the other."

In 1942, Mom's folks had moved to northern Alabama, where Pa Bradley had found work on the Wilson Dam, a TVA project. Dad and Mom were there when I was born in the Helen Keller Hospital on August 19 of that year. (Over half a century later, I learned that the year before, my colleague Senator Mitch McConnell of Kentucky had also been born in that hospital. They probably would have shut the place down if they had known that they were producing that many senators—and in that day, even more alarming, Republican senators, to boot.)

Fletch

IN THE FALL of 1942, Dad found work "up north" in Cleveland, Ohio, driving a big trailer-truck rig. The boss asked him if he'd ever driven a truck like that. He replied that he was "born in a truck just like that." Of course, he'd never seen one before. He got the job. When I was a few months old, Mom took me to Cleveland on a train, and we lived in a small apartment while Dad was on the road.

When Dad would meet someone named Thompson, and the subject came up as to whether he and the stranger might be related, Dad would invariably say, "Could be—my daddy was a traveling man." In truth, it was Dad who was the traveling man—at heart, anyway. He would often say that driving a big rig in New England was the most fun of his life. He was twenty-two, World War II had started, and he was hauling airplane parts over icy roads. He and a buddy would take turns driving and sleeping in the back of the cab. The wheels never stopped rolling. He would laugh and tell stories about the adventures of himself and other country boys who'd gone north to find work, and of his days on the road at truck stops when they were all indestructible and invisible. Once he was sitting on a stool with his back to the door, and someone came in the door and said, "I can whip any SOB that ever came out of Tennessee," and he put down his drink, ready to fight, and was face-to-face with an old friend from Tennessee, laughing like the devil. Or the time he left his buddy asleep in the cab while he pulled in for a cup of coffee. The truck was parked close to the highway, and when the guy woke up bleary-eyed and heard the traffic, he assumed that they were still rolling. When he glanced down and saw that no one was in the driver's seat, he almost tore up the cab trying to get behind the wheel. Of course, these were just the stories Dad could tell his kids.

If these were the best of times for Dad (behind the wheel of an eighteen-wheeler instead of a Tennessee mule), they were the worst of times for Mom, a country girl a long way from home. She stayed scared for one reason or another for the entire two and a half years we were there in Ohio. We lived in a little apartment surrounded by people who talked funny—at least to this country girl who had never been away from home. Thoughtfully, Dad's truck-driving buddies would tell Mom tales of Dad's daredevil exploits behind the wheel, like the time he was flying down an icy hill and saw a jackknifed truck wrecked at the bottom of the hill, blocking the highway and making passage impossible. At least the buddy thought it was impossible. Rather than take the ditch or apply the brakes, Dad went on through with inches to spare.

When I was a little boy and we would meet a big rig on the highway, Dad would often raise his fist up and make a pulling-down motion. Sure enough, to my delight, the driver would pull down on his horn and give a loud blast. Looking back, I can almost hear Dad thinking, "Enjoy it, son. It's better than you think."

Naturally, his attitude toward such things found its way into his vast catalog of irreverent comments in later years. When I started driving and was getting ready to go on a little trip, three things would invariably be said. First, Mom would tell me to be careful and not drive too fast. Then Dad would say, "You better *not* let anybody pass you, son." Then she'd say, "FLETCHER."

Every man needs a time of adventure in his life, no matter how brief. It gives him something to relate to—something to remind him that he hasn't been cheated. He can relive it and mold it to fit his needs. I think that's what trucking in a "foreign land" in dangerous times did for Dad.

However, after almost three years, it was time to go home to Lawrenceburg. After we relocated, Dad knocked around for a while before he found his true calling. He drove a "muck truck," hauling this delicate mixture of dirt and whatever to construction sites. He drove a bus that carried workers to a chemical plant in Mt. Pleasant, and he did a few other things before he apparently decided that wheels were his thing. He opened a little used-car lot in Lawrenceburg, and that's the way he made his living for pretty much the remainder of his life. His getting started wasn't that complicated. He did it without any help from his folks, an SBA loan, a "stimulus grant," or anything else. He had all he needed—a good reputation at the bank. He was known to be a fellow who paid his debts. He'd borrow some money, take two or three boys with him to the auto sale in Nashville, buy a few cars, drive them bank to Lawrenceburg, and put them on the lot.

He didn't have the opportunity to travel much later on, but every once in a while he and Mom would take off on the open road—often heading "out west." Once, when I was still in single digits, we drove to Arizona, quite a trip in those days. It was Mom, Dad, me, and two new 1949 Chevys. We towed the other one with a trailer hitch, as Dad intended to sell it somewhere along the way. As it turned out, we came back with the same two Chevys.

I may not have been the best traveler in the world. Years later, when I heard a joke on TV about a kid on a family trip bugging his dad with "Are we there yet?," I thought, à la Seinfeld, "Wait a minute, I *invented* 'Are we there yet?'" This was long before the time when I thought the desert was beautiful. There were no places to stop, and I didn't like the warm water we drank from a canvas canteen we had tied to the bumper to keep it "cool." In these pre-air-conditioning days, we couldn't really drive with the windows either up or down for more than a minute. Dad was loving it. Mom was tolerating it. I was miserable. As Dad would say, "Other than that, everything was fine." And I'm sure I hid my discomfort well and was cheerful throughout.

As a gentle lesson to parents who may be overly optimistic as to the educational benefits of travel for young boys, I can state that I remember two things about the trip. First, it was long. Second, I saw the grave of Pat Garrett, the sheriff who shot Billy the Kid.

Having said that, I can't really say that I gave the trip a fair shot. You can't see that much scenery when you're lying down in the backseat with a comic book. Yes, my sense of adventure along with the rest of me lay dormant, while my sense of wonder was limited to seeking frequent updates as to our exact location and how long it was to lunch. Not improving my disposition was the fact that in my attempts to gather intelligence from the front seat, I had to take care to frame my inquiries carefully to avoid a Fletcherism designed to infuriate. If I asked, "Where are we now, Daddy?," he would invariably reply, "Right along here, son." It was information that was technically correct and totally useless. Like a lot of the stuff I was learning in school, I figured.

Since time began, the trader and the merchant have had to develop the necessary skills to survive—and Dad was no different. He had to have a pretty good eye for what a car would "bring" when he bought it at auction. There wasn't much margin for error. He could look at a car across a lot and tell whether it was previously wrecked or whether it was a "northern" car, meaning it was driven on snowy, icy roads strewn with salt and therefore more likely to rust. He also had a pretty good idea about a car's odometer reading. If he knew the seller of a car he had bought, he would add to the list of selling points "original miles."

There were few impediments or requirements for getting into the car business, and it seemed that every horse-trading country boy in Lawrence County who did not want to work for "the man" opened a used-car lot—for a while, anyway. Competition was heavy, and I sometimes wondered how Dad competed with folks who sold old beat-up rattletraps with odometer readings worthy of a little old lady who drove only on Sundays. Did he fight fire with fire, so to speak? I didn't really want to know. All I know is that he sold used cars in the same little town for forty years. More than once a young fellow would walk onto the lot and say, "Mr. Thompson, my dad bought his first car from you and he said that I should, too." That told me all I needed to know.

As I was growing up, Dad traded houses the way he traded cars—as often as possible. The trouble was, they were houses we were living in. He would build a house and we would move into it. He would be offered a little profit, sell the house, and then we'd rent and repeat the process all over again. We must have lived in half the houses in town, and Mom used to say, "I've cleaned up about every old house in this town." To Dad, whether it was a car or a house, it was just good business.

Dad would also move his place of business from time to time. Some of his car lots had "offices." The office usually consisted of a little two-room structure with a portable fan and checkerboard. The great issues of the day were resolved there, especially political issues: If the issues couldn't be handled over the checkerboard, they were taken to the Blue Ribbon Café, where even more learned experts would weigh in. But Fletch's place was always the place where a fellow could have a good laugh, listen to some Hank Williams on the radio, play some checkers—and maybe kick a few tires and test the car market. I remember one fellow called "Shorty," who was well named and had a big potbelly. He was a fixture at both the lot and at the Blue Ribbon. He was in the insurance business, and dressed well, always wearing a necktie with his short-sleeve shirt and straw hat. However, his claim to fame was his ability to quickly suck in his stomach and cause his pants to fall to the floor. "Never know when the unexpected is going to happen," he would tell his startled customers. He sold a lot of policies with that one. Shorty understood marketing.

Dad had always been drawn to politics and had grown up

a Democrat. Pa Thompson never voted for a Republican in his life and thought that FDR had saved their lives. In later years they laughed and talked about, during the Great Depression, eating a thin gruel called "Hoover gravy," named after President Hoover. Politics was a matter of looking out for the "little man." And in rural Middle Tennessee in the 1930s, my folks were very "little" from an economic standpoint. When Dad would take me to the barbershop when I was five or six years old, he would say, "Tell them what you are, son." He had coached me to say "a Democrat." It was probably my first lesson on how to get a laugh.

However, by the 1950s, politics in Lawrenceburg were not a matter of ideology or party policies. It was a matter of the ins and outs. The outs wanted to be in, and the ins did not want to be out. The Democrats controlled the local and county political machinery and the patronage that went with it. That was basically a holdover from the Civil War. In Tennessee you could almost tell the politics of the county by the lay of the land. In mountainous East Tennessee, where slavery was rare and several counties never did secede from the Union, it was heavily Republican. As you got over to the rolling hills of Middle Tennessee, including Lawrenceburg, and especially West Tennessee, where the terrain became flatter, it became cotton country and was Democratic. In Lawrence County, since there were not enough Republicans to succeed as a party, some independents and some disgruntled Democrats formed a "coalition" party. Dad was a coalition man.

The coalition ticket gradually gained some traction in county politics, where voters determined who controlled the courthouse and the main offices, such as sheriff, trustee, county court clerk, circuit court clerk, and county register. During election season, rallies would be held in every community in the county. Little country-music bands would play as the speechifying of politicians filled the hot night air and vice versa. It seemed that the energy and acrimony expended were in inverse proportion to the importance of the office. It was amazing to me how much excitement could be generated over the burning question of who was going to be elected to register deeds at the courthouse for the next four years.

The group most interested in these elections were the free-market purveyors of illegal spirits, otherwise known as bootleggers. And they were interested in only one job: sheriff. Whether or not a sheriff was going to be broad-minded with regard to their business endeavors was of primary importance to these folks. It was always assumed—and occasionally proven—that they ensured this broad-mindedness with a little money from time to time, and I am not just speaking of campaign contributions. In fact, over the years the relationship between some of the county sheriffs and the bootleggers was more of a partnership than anything else. So it made for heated campaigns and plenty of "walking-around money" on Election Day.

All of this, of course, was well known to the coalition coffee drinkers at the Blue Ribbon Café, whose owner, Dudley Brewer, was the town's leading and most respected Republican. The coalition had never elected a sheriff, and they needed to nominate someone whom people liked, was preferably honest, and who looked plausible standing behind the badge. Fletch was their man.

Initially, Dad's biggest hurdle as a potential candidate was explaining to Mom how the sheriff lived "*in* the jail," as Mom would put it, or "*at* the jail," as Dad described it. Dad saw it as a terrific rent-free benefit and pretty exciting. The ancient two-story brick building on the edge of town looked like Davy Crockett had built it, or perhaps Davy Crockett's father. The jail cells were on the second floor, and the sheriff's family and offices were on the first floor. Dad never did really understand why Mom didn't think this was a great setup. She wouldn't even have to clean it up. Carefully selected criminals would do that for her. In one of life's little ironies, it was the same jail where Dad had lost his tooth to that deputy sheriff many years prior. Dad thought his longstanding ties to the building might be a strong selling point for voters, though Mom persuaded him that it wasn't funny and probably wasn't a good idea to bring up on the campaign trail.

As always, Dad finally sold Mom on his idea, but alas

not to enough voters. He made a good run against a well-entrenched incumbent. It turned out to be a bad year for the coalition, but the campaign did give me some time with Dad. I drove him around the back roads of the county in search of votes. When he would see someone sitting in a rocker on their front porch, we would stop for a spell. The problem was that they usually would know Fletch and he would talk with them as long as they wanted to. Dad enjoyed it and was buoyed by the fact that everybody he saw and talked to was for him—which, of course, is every beginning politician's delusion. To make matters worse, we were only seeing a handful of people every day on our trips.

Occasionally, Mom would hear a disparaging word, but it was often along the lines of "Fletch is too good of a man to be sheriff." It aggravated Dad, but I knew that Mom agreed. At the supper table at night, Dad would talk about what a great thing it would be to help clean up politics in Lawrence County and the way he would elevate the sheriff's office in the eyes of the people. Over the years, I decided that it probably was a good thing that this political neophyte full of high ideals was never confronted with the reality of the sheriff's office in Lawrence County. Besides the bad influences of the office, Dad was a little naïve when it came to people. His talent for driving a hard bargain, his wicked sense of humor, and his occasional flashes of temper concealed a soft heart; he was a sucker for a hard-luck story. Every miscreant caught redhanded by the law who protested his innocence and any ne'er-do-well or drunk who insisted they were a "changed man" found a willing believer in Fletcher Thompson. In retrospect, the bootleggers and a majority of the voters were probably right. Not a good fit.

Years later, Dad's friendship with Pat Sutton said a lot about Dad and the nature of Lawrence County politics. Dad had become friendly with Sutton when he ran for and was elected to Congress representing the district that Lawrence County was in. He was a smart, good-looking guy with an outgoing personality, and in fact he looked a lot like Dad. Dad thought he was great. After a few years in Congress, Sutton took on the popular Senator Estes Kefauver. Kefauver beat him badly, and Sutton left the area for several years. He returned to Lawrence County with great fanfare and ran for county sheriff and won. In 1964 he was charged in a counterfeiting conspiracy—that's right, a rural county sheriff charged with counterfeiting. Even more bizarre, he persuaded the people that it was all a conspiracy between the FBI (which does not have counterfeiting jurisdiction) and his local political opponents. He was reelected. Dad supported him all the way (even after he was convicted).

The day after Dad's own election defeat, he was back on the car lot. On the surface, at least, there was no keeping Fletch's spirits down. By Christmas he was in rare form. At Ma and Pa Bradley's house in Tuscumbia, Alabama, by tradition the entire extended family, each with a passel of kids, would sit around the living room and open presents one at a time, starting with the youngest. All of Mom's sisters and her brother and their spouses had opened their gifts one after the other, working up to the eldest. Each couple was opening their gifts and was receiving an envelope from Ma and Pa Bradley containing a $100 bill. Thanks, oohs and aahs all around. Mom being the oldest sibling, she and Dad opened their envelope from Ma and Pa Bradley last. Dad had the honors. Out of the envelope came not one but two $100 bills. Dad, trying to look slightly embarrassed, held up the two $100 bills for all to see, thanking Ma and Pa Bradley profusely. Ma Bradley almost died. For a moment everyone was looking at one another or at the floor—until they saw Dad grinning. Then it hit them. He had slipped the second $100 bill into the envelope. The entire family was doubled over in laughter for thirty minutes.

Dad could hold his own in any company. I invited Mom and Dad to D.C. during the Watergate hearings and introduced him to my friend, Connie Valanos, the owner of the Monocle Restaurant, a landmark on Capitol Hill where I spent many evenings. Connie was a humorous guy himself, and he and Dad struck up a friendship. One night when Mom and Dad walked into the restaurant, Connie said to Dad, "Fletcher, was that your briefcase left in here last night with ten thousand dollars in it?" Dad immediately replied, "Yeah, but it was twenty thousand."

. . .

Being "Fletch's boy" gave me the benefit of the doubt growing up in Lawrenceburg. And I often needed it. While Dad
had a temper and could say angry things to me in the heat of
the moment, I could count on my folks to be there for me
day in and day out. The more trouble I would get into and
the worse my offense, the calmer Dad became. He never
punished me when he saw that I was punishing myself. As a
little boy, I simply worshiped him. He was not one for much
small talk or "activities," but I simply thought he could do
anything.

Kids are shaped by what they can take for granted. I knew
that Mom would come in at bedtime (after dutiful applica-
tion of face cream and hair net) and we would say our prayers
together (although I never really took to that "and if I should
die before I wake" part). I knew that Mom and Dad would
be together and always there for me. It produced a childhood
without one moment's insecurity or anguish over anything
going on in my home.

To one extent or another, every man measures himself
against his father. Once past the adulation phase and the resentment phase, something more realistic sets in. You begin
to think, "I remember Dad at this age—at the age I am now."
It's only then that I realize that he did not have everything
figured out at times when I thought he was so strong and
certain.

My parents never set the bar high for me as far as education or professional titles were concerned. But they gave me much more. Dad set the standard for what a man ought to be—strong and protective of those who depended on him. Trustworthy and striving every day to be a better man. It became a standard by which I measured things, whether I lived up to them or not.

Eager Little
Minds . . . and Me

OUR PRIMARY CATHEDRAL of public learning in Lawrenceburg was imaginatively named Lawrenceburg Public School. It was the beginning of the educational journey for many enthusiastic, lovable little tykes eager to learn. There were also some kids like me.

In his "Intimations of Immortality," Wordsworth writes of the innocent insight of children, uncomplicated and uncorrupted by the world. He obviously never met Mrs. Maude's first-grade class—or Mrs. Maude, for that matter. Human survival instincts kick in at a very early age, and for an obstreperous lad in Mrs. Maude's room, pain aversion was the highest priority. There are any number of things that might assault the senses or the dignity of the untamed first-grader, such as a steely-eyed warning, a verbal lashing, or the paddle. Therefore, strategies were needed. As the year wore on and I developed more sophistication, I learned that if my offense was not too severe, instead of a paddling Mrs. Maude would banish me to the cloakroom. That, of course, was like throwing Br'er Rabbit into the briar patch. I would take an adequate number of coats off the hook, make myself a bed and a pillow, and take a nap. I missed much class participation this way, but my absence seemed to be a sacrifice that Mrs. Maude was often willing to make.

They say that school inspires certain precocious kids to set goals early in life. This was certainly true of me. Every day my goal was to get the heck out of school and get back home as soon as possible.

Over the next several months, I stoically muddled my way through. Actually, Lawrenceburg Public was not all that bad. It was a medium-security facility with home-visitation privileges, and when the food was too bad, with the cunning of a seasoned inmate, I always had ways of disposing of it. Spinach served at lunch could be slipped off the plate and into the pocket, later to be transferred to the book satchel and taken home. Displaying, even then, a rank inability to cover up my misdeeds, I would usually forget about the spinach and have to explain to my mother once again how the spinach accidentally found its way into the book satchel. It was the most consistent exercise of my imagination.

All things considered, it was a fairly typical, sometimes tension-filled, but more often carefree few years. I was able to get a few laughs, draw some pretty good cartoons, and even learn a number of things. As time rolled on, a pudgy, little uninterested Freddie Thompson grew to become a taller, slimmer uninterested Freddie Thompson, who wondered why the teachers always looked at him when something went wrong. Perhaps it was because I was the one who turned on the fire alarm one day and caused the entire school to bolt out onto the playground. Who knows? Occasionally, I was even innocent, so I resented being picked on.

Kids are introduced to the real grown-up world through their grade-school teachers, and I had the full array of heroines and villains, at least in my youthful eyes. I still remember one moment of supreme validation. I'd told my mother that my black-haired third-grade teacher, who was immune to my charms, looked like an old black rooster. Sometime later in the year, my mom came home laughing. She'd been to a parent-teacher conference, and as she was talking to this teacher, it dawned on her that my description fit her to a tee; it was all she could do to keep from breaking up in laughter. Of course, Mom was making a terrible mistake by telling me this, but I loved her dearly for it.

My penchant for horseplay was exceeded only by my ineptitude. On one occasion when I thought no one was looking and the class was being led down the steps to lunch, I proceeded to stomp each step as I descended, creating the noise that was intended. My teacher was waiting at the bottom and yelled, "Freddie!" I immediately replied, "I wasn't stomping the steps."

I had a wonderful fourth-grade teacher, Mrs. Jackson. She actually laughed at some of the funny things I would say.

(Even then, this was the way I judged a woman.) However, unbeknownst to her, she totally screwed up my sense of direction forever. She had this huge map of the United States hung on the wall. Of course, we were taught that "up" on the map was north. The problem was that the map was hung on the south wall of the classroom, the direction of Ma and Pa Bradley's home in Tuscumbia, Alabama. So for years when I visualized the location of a state, I did it by thinking of the map in the classroom. When I related it to the real world, like on a trip to my grandparents' house, in my mind north was actually south. I don't have to tell you what that did to east and west. Of course, the lesson I took away from this at the time was that stuff you learned in the classroom didn't really apply to the real world.

Perhaps of interest to educators the world over is the fact that the only thing I remember from the fifth grade is that, once a day, Mrs. Newton would read to us from a Nancy Drew mystery. I became absorbed in these stories even to the extent of checking some additional ones out of the library. It was probably the first time I had actually read anything in order to get information. I wanted to know what was going to happen next. I had to smile years later when I heard Supreme Court Justice O'Connor and Supreme Court nominee Sotomayor talk about how, as young girls, this smart, courageous young Nancy Drew inspired them with an example of a girl capable of doing great things. So it seems that

Nancy Drew inspired Freddie Thompson and many young girls everywhere. Young Fred would have been mighty chagrined to know that. He didn't think about the boy-girl stuff. He just wanted to know what was in the "old clock."

While I was still in grade school I decided I needed to have my own "walking-around money." I figured that a fellow never knows when he will run across a business deal that he can't afford to pass up. Besides, I thought it was past time for me to be able to flash a roll of bills like they do in the movies. So I found a job as a carhop at the local Dairy Dip, the main (and only) drive-in hot spot in town. Although I was basically working for tips, the Dairy Dip, with its heavy traffic, could make me a killing, I figured. The only problem was that the Dip, as advertised, had wonderful hot dogs and shakes, and employees did not get a discount. You can see where this is going. So, although I made a few bucks every night in tips, I was eating more in hot dogs, shakes, and other stuff than I was bringing in. I had become not only an employee of the Dairy Dip but one of its best customers, and I was losing money on the deal.

Actually, that wasn't the only problem. I worked the last shift at night, which meant that I had to pick up and sweep the entire lot clean every night after we closed—a job the early-shift carhops got to skip. After several weeks of this, I began to question my negotiating and business acumen. I believe that's the first time the phrase "Surely there's a better way" occurred to me. I left that job older and wiser (and fatter), with a bad taste in my mouth for hot dogs that lasted for about five years.

During my last years in grade school I may not have been raking in the dough, but I was racking up significant time in the principal's office for an array of minor offenses. The principal's outpost was manned by a middle-aged gentleman who always seemed to be remarkably cheerful. My daddy had always said that a man who walks around with a smile on his face all the time can't possibly know what's going on. Nevertheless, he was funny and I liked him. Besides, I didn't want him to know everything that was going on.

At assembly one day during a magazine sales drive to raise money for the school (no, I didn't sell any magazines), he got on stage and announced that he was not going to wash his feet until we met our sales quota. Everyone laughed uproariously. Great stuff. Unfortunately, he was also what we called "country strong"—something I learned the first time he paddled my rear end and lifted me off the ground. The man had leverage. I never could figure out how such a nice guy could hit so hard. But I knew I didn't have much to complain about. They say that the professional criminal is caught only about one out of eight times he commits an offense. I figured that was about right.

Boyhood is a series of second chances. In Lawrenceburg it was not based on social or economic standing. It was based on who your parents were, which determined whether you were basically a "good kid" even when you gave every indication that you were not. One preteen night while our parents were visiting at my house, a buddy and I walked down the street and behind Dudley Brewer's café. There was a big window fan in the back that cooled the café's kitchen area. We thought it would be a great idea to fill a bottle with water and fling the water into the fan, causing those inside to get a shower. I was the gunner on this mission. I slung the water from the bottle and started running. I heard breaking glass but assumed that it was the water bottle breaking. We ran home, laughing about the now-wet café patrons. We sat down in my yard and were talking when Mr. Brewer walked up. The sound I heard of glass breaking was not the bottle, as I had supposed, but the window that the bottle had gone through. We explained and apologized, but Mr. Brewer was not amused. He gave us a lecture, and as he walked away my heart sank.

Over the next few days, I waited for the guy who owned and ran the restaurant where Dad had coffee every day to spill the beans. It never happened. Finally, my conscience got the best of me and I told Dad. He went to Mr. Brewer to make amends, and I never knew exactly how it was resolved, but since Dad never mentioned it again, my guess is that Mr. Brewer refused payment for the window.

Fifteen years later, Mr. Brewer still owned and operated

the Blue Ribbon Café and was still the respected titular head of the Republican Party in the county. When I came back to practice law, he took me under his wing and gave me calm guidance and support. He didn't remember that incident with the scared little boy to whom he had decided to give a break several years earlier. But I did.

ABOVE: Lawrence County High School—the scene of many schoolboy crimes. (*Lawrence County Archives*) RIGHT: Lawrence County Courthouse, with Davy standing watch. (*Lawrence County Archives*) BELOW: The town square in Lawrenceburg. (*Lawrence County Archives*)

RIGHT: Mom, Dad, and me in Cleveland, Ohio, 1943.
BELOW: Pa and Ma Thompson with Dad and Uncle Mitch behind them, with Uncles Wayne and Dallas at either end.

TOP LEFT: Dad during truck-driving days. TOP RIGHT: Checking out the truck. Me at age three. ABOVE: Dad on the car lot on a slow, snowy day in 1966.

ABOVE: The Roaring Lions undefeated (before the season started), with me at age thirteen (top row, right end). BELOW: Doing what rascals do: leading my cousin Butch astray.

LEFT: Sixteen years old and trying to develop that sly-dog look. BELOW: At seventeen.

ABOVE: The 1959 L.C.H.S. basketball team. I'm the second from the right in the top row, and my fighting buddy Joe Plunkett is on the left end in the same row. BELOW: Five generations: Tony, me, Mom, Grandma Bradley, and Great-Grandma Sealy.

ABOVE: Dan, Tony, and Betsy in 1967, the year we moved back to Lawrenceburg, where I began to practice law. BELOW: Meeting Reagan before a speech in Jackson, Tennessee, in 1968. RIGHT: Dad, brother Ken, and me after the "Marie" trial, which led me to the movies.

LEFT: Dad taking it easy. ABOVE: Lawrenceburg the day I announced my Senate run, with lawyer buddy Jim Weatherford, the victim of one of my better practical jokes. BELOW: Dan, Betsy, and Tony, all grown up.

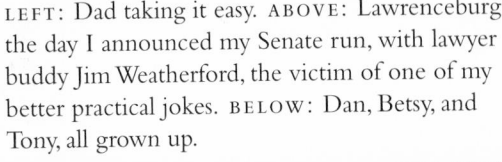

Gimme That
Ole-Time Religion

I GUESS I WAS a "strict constructionist" at an early age. Of course, this term, when applied to the Constitution, means that the Constitution means what it says. It should be interpreted as much as possible according to the plain meaning of the document and the original intent of its framers.

In the Church of Christ, we wholeheartedly agreed with this concept. Except it was the Bible that was to be strictly construed. And the original intent was that of God Himself. It was pretty simple, really. You did what the Bible told you, and you followed the example of the early Christians. The scriptures told us to believe, repent, and be baptized. As a kid, while I had considerable difficulties with the English language in school, I learned at least one word of Greek— *baptizo,* which means "immersion." When you got baptized, you were immersed in the water. The scriptures definitely did not refer to being "sprinkled," a risky if not damnable shortcut. So, at the age of thirteen, without notice to my parents, I walked down the aisle one Wednesday night and was baptized.

By the same token, the early Christians were told to sing and make melody in their hearts. There was no mention of instrumental music. So we had none. Neither did we have a choir. Referring to the invidious creeping in of modern technology that preachers often use nowadays, my wife, Jeri, once asked me where the biblical authority was for overhead projectors. I told her not to be a smart aleck.

Every Church of Christ was self-sufficient and independent. The elders of each church elected the preacher and supervised the flock. We had fellowship with other congregations but no centralized authority, regional council, or conference to answer to. It was the next step past "federalism," I suppose—perhaps a little more like the Articles of Confederation.

When it came to personal conduct, the admonitions were equally straightforward. The Ten Commandments were featured along, of course, with the teachings of Jesus. I had no problems with the Ten Commandments. They didn't seem to address anything that I wanted to do at that early age anyway. However, I paid especially close attention to other parts of the Old Testament. Clearly, God was someone I did not want to mess with.

At the First Street Church of Christ, the message from the pulpit was not subtle. For years I had no idea what the preacher was talking about, but I knew that it was serious business. Having picked up on the hellfire and damnation part, I remember wanting to be just good enough to avoid it. There was a Heaven and there was a Hell, and the preacher could explain in excruciating detail why Hell was not the better choice. Needless to say, from the time I was a small boy, the Bible teachings and the charismatic preachers I heard on Sundays made a distinct impression on me. I wanted to be a good boy and I most certainly didn't want to go to Hell. The only real doubt I had about matters of religion, as a child, was the part about living forever when you went to Heaven. Since that is where I planned to go, I had to figure out what it would be like, and I could never get my mind around the concept of living forever. Living in Heaven for ten thousand years was like you'd just begun, the old gospel song went. I dwelled upon "What is forever like?" and Mom did her best to explain. I suppose she wondered, "What kind of an oddball kid do I have on my hands here? He is not worried about dying or going to Hell. He is worried about going to Heaven." I resolved this theological crisis in my own mind by deciding that when I got to Heaven, it would all be explained to me. And, anyway, I would be happy because that is what you are in Heaven.

Church doctrine also did not allow for dancing. The joke among the teenagers was that the Church of Christ kids couldn't go to the dance, so they just had to go "parking" instead. There was more than a little truth to that.

My family was there every time the church doors were open. Sunday-morning Sunday school, then the main church service, then again on Sunday night. Then on Wednesday nights for Bible study. On Sunday mornings, I sat there bleary-eyed with stains of shoe polish on my fingers, in a white shirt with a collar at least two sizes too small and a necktie with a knot my daddy taught me how to tie—the half Windsor, the only knot I ever learned to tie and the one I use today. My eyes were usually firmly fixed on the clock on the wall, but I did pick up a few things. For example, in Sunday school I learned that the gospel meant "good news." I kept waiting for it.

After services, while the kids ran, played, and occasionally fought in the yard in the front of the church, the men would light up and the women would visit. Whatever social stratification there was in town disappeared at church. I can recall one of Dad's friends was always trying to get himself and his family invited over to our house for Sunday dinner after services, a notion that Dad was less then enthusiastic about. Half kidding, he'd invariably say, "Fletch, what are you having for dinner?" Dad would always reply, "Company." And that would be the end of it.

At the time, what I thought was one of the most significant moments of my youth occurred after church one Wednesday night when I tangled with a kid from my Bible class. Joe Plunkett was one year older than I was and as tough as a nail. In high school, we played football and basketball on the varsity together, worked as lifeguards together, and off and on for those four years went at each other when the necessity arose. It seemed like the natural thing to do. That Wednesday night I received a black eye, but Joe cried. I considered that I clearly got the best of the deal, and more important, Dad seemed to think so too.

As I mentioned, I found it pretty easy to be a good boy because I had no interest in stealing, telling any (major) lies, or coveting my neighbor's wife, whatever that meant—or even dancing, for that matter. Occasionally, I had reason to wonder if it might be harder to keep the faith when I grew up. Usually, it had to do with listening to some of the older boys behind the church after services were over. It was sort of a celebration that they had survived another church service, as they laughed and joked. For example: Moses came down from the mountain and said, "Boys I've got good news and bad news. The good news is I got him down to ten. The bad news is adultery is still in." I laughed hard. And I secretly thought I should find out what the heck they were talking about.

Actually, the sins of the flesh were relevant in more than one way during my boyhood church days. I remember, as a very young boy, the hushed whispers about the preacher who had inspired my folks to join the church but later partook of the forbidden fruit in the form of one of the church ladies.

The lesson of the need to separate the man from the message stood me in good stead years later when we learned that the preacher, a good friend of our family who had married my high school sweetheart and me, was convicted of transporting stolen tractors across state lines. (I also recall that my telling her straight-faced that his conviction invalidated our marriage fell pretty flat.) It seemed that we were getting a little more than our share of public virtue and private vice right from our own pulpit. It occurred to me later on, however—what better preparation for politics?

A lesson the political class could have learned from our church's elders was the policy of rotating out our preachers every few years. On one occasion when one of our preachers was told by the elders that his services would not be retained the following year, he got up in the pulpit the next Sunday morning and basically said, with a quivering voice, that the Lord and most of the flock wanted him to be in Lawrenceburg and therefore he was refusing to leave. This of course was heresy, but he did have many supporters enamored of him—we called it "preacheritis." There were angry exchanges among the parishoners and threats of fisticuffs in the churchyard before this would-be revolution against the elders was put down. However, it did result in a split in the church, with the preacher and his followers forming a new church closer to town. As far as we were concerned, this kind of preacher was memorialized in a song by Charlie Daniels years later when he sang, "Jesus walked on the water and I know that it's true. Sometimes I think that preacher man would like to do a little walking too." Soon our little congregation, having been purified though diminished in size, was back to normal. Some of our friends in the more "sophisticated" Catholic and Presbyterian churches, with whom we carried on constant good-natured, if serious, arguments over doctrine, referred to our congregation, after our split, as the poorer of the two congregations. One of their more clever blasphemers was heard to say, "Their church is so poor that their members have to bring their own snakes on Sunday."

Actually, the policy of rotating the preacher every few years seemed to work quite well. It kept the congregation from becoming too attached to any one personality, and it kept the preachers on their toes, knowing that they'd need a good recommendation for their next job. This was my first encounter with term limits. And it made good sense to me. The fact that neither politicians nor preachers seemed to like the idea also appealed to me.

Mom and Dad enjoyed having a good time, and people especially gravitated to Dad's humor. Preachers were no exception. (Perhaps the possibility of getting a good deal on a used car didn't hurt the relationship, either.) For the most part, these preachers were good men having to move their families from pillar to post in order to preach the gospel. Many of them were exceptional orators, which Dad admired. Several even had a good sense of humor. They and their families were often at our house for cookouts and ice cream made from a hand-cranked freezer. They would match my dad story for story, recounting tales from their days on the road, like the time one preacher was invited over to a family's house for Sunday dinner and saw Grandma, who was carrying a lower lip full of snuff, inadvertently drop a big load of it into the batch of coleslaw that she was preparing. He said he hadn't had coleslaw since.

As I look back on those early Lawrenceburg years growing up in what some might call a fundamentalist church, I am struck by how much has stayed with me and become a part of the way that I view life, even after my "enlightened" years as a philosophy major in college and my sojourns in Washington, Hollywood, and New York. It doesn't have so much to do with doctrine, and it certainly did not always keep me on the straight and narrow path. But my early lessons had penetrated pretty deep and had an irritating way of reasserting themselves at inconvenient times.

On a more fundamental level, the notion of sin and redemption sums up the story of mankind. We can rise to great heights ethically and morally, and we can achieve great accomplishments. There are hard-and-fast rules that we can hold on to in a constantly changing world, but we are prone to err and "miss the mark." We must constantly work at doing the right thing.

The most important things that you learn as a child are the things that you don't realize that you're learning. And in my case, in later years, much of this had political significance for me. Man's weaknesses made necessary the checks and balances our founders were wise enough to see were needed in our system of government. This insight also gave us our system of federalism. Power in the hands of man must be dispersed. One does not have to be sold on the concept of original sin in order to conclude that we should all be more than a little modest with regard to most human endeavors. Mistakes, miscalculations, and corruption have too often accompanied the ambitions of individuals as well as governments. The nature of man and the principles that had survived the ages seemed to me to be a much more reliable yardstick than the fads and intellectual brainstorms of the day. For me, this was the essence of conservatism and still is.

Perhaps surprisingly to some, having political views based on childhood religious influences does not necessarily translate into approval of a lot of the political activities of some religious groups. In our church, we drew a clear distinction between the responsibilities of church and state. This was not a legal concept. It was one based upon scripture: "Render unto Caesar . . ." Jesus and the apostles were not social activists or community organizers. They were in the business of saving souls and changing hearts and minds. I found no historical evidence of the early churches organizing to change any law. To the best of my knowledge, no fund-raising scrolls have been unearthed. Their goals were much more important than that. In all those years growing up, I don't recall hearing one political reference ever coming from the pulpit. Members could do what they thought they should do in politics, but that was not the role of the church. Neither did the church, as such, have social welfare responsibilities. Oh, to be sure, helping one's fellow man was encouraged, but it was an individual's responsibility. As one old-timer put it, "If you want to join the Lions Club, they're down the road. We're about something different here."

Sounds a little harsh perhaps, but in this day of mega-churches and attempts by the Left and the Right to involve their churches in activities far removed from the original role of the church, it still has resonance for that boy who shined those pews with his Sunday pants while he (mostly) watched the clock many years ago.

Pooch

THERE ARE FEW THINGS more heartwarming to a man than his memories of that special dog he had growing up. Romping through the fields together, playing catch, hunting birds—best pals. My fondest recollection of my dog is nothing like that. Don't get me wrong, my dog and I had our joyous moments, as well as melancholy ones. However, when I think of him, the thought is often accompanied not by just a smile but by a laugh. And, as was so often the case, it is based on something my dad did to the utter chagrin of my sainted mother.

The story starts with a car trade. Dad was getting close to a deal when he focused on the dog sitting in the backseat. "It's a deal if you throw in the dog," he said. "Done," the man replied. So I had a new dog. His name was Pooch. Obviously, his original owner had put a lot of thought into naming the dog, and it seemed to suit him fine. He was a pooch and looked like a pooch. He was a pretty big dog and looked to be part hound, long and lanky, and part bulldog, with kind of a squished-up face but with long ears and a tongue that almost hit the ground. He was white with large black spots, and he was a beautiful sight as he loped along.

At the time, Dad was a salesman at Caperton Chevrolet and was doing pretty well. He built a house on Caperton Avenue, which was the street that the boss lived on, although at the other end of the street in a much larger house. As always, our circumstances reflected the vicissitudes of the economy and the car business, and this was a little more up-scale than the houses we usually had. We bought a TV but we had no air-conditioning, so on hot summer nights we would put the TV in the window and watch it through the screen as we sat in the yard. In other words, we were thoroughly enjoying our new neighborhood. Little did we know that scandal was about to upset it all.

One summer day, Dad was painting our metal lawn chairs in the front yard. Painting them a bright yellow. Pooch was irritating him by being especially frisky, running around the yard and occasionally brushing up against the chair that Dad was painting. Pooch had just made a pass by the chair and Dad, with his brush dripping with paint, reflexively took a swipe at Pooch with the brush. He missed him—well, most of him; he actually swiped Pooch from behind and right between his legs. Specifically, he painted Pooch's more than ample testicles a bright yellow. Pooch jogged off oblivious and happy, his newly luminous endowments swinging from side to side. Pooch always had the run of the neighborhood. Normally you could see him coming, but now you could *really* see him going from about a half mile away. My mother was apoplectic. First it was "What in the world is wrong with Pooch?"—thinking he had contracted some deadly disease. Then, when she was informed what had happened, it was "Fletcher, you have got to catch that dog."

"Yeah, and then what?" he replied.

Good question. He did not want to be the one to try to apply the paint remover. There was only one thing for Mom to do. Since Pooch was well known in the neighborhood as "the Thompson dog," she would not show her face until "that stuff wore off."

I, of course, thought it was the neatest thing to have everybody talking about my dog. Dad acted like he was chagrined just like Mom, but later I wondered if the paintbrush incident had really been an accident. All I know is that a few years later, when the movie came out about a boy and his dog named "Old Yeller," it had a special meaning for me.

The Movie Star Club

OR ME, A GREAT DAY was getting to go to what we called "the show"—that is, the Crockett Theater (down the street from the Crockett Gas Station, across from the Crockett Beauty Salon, and on the way to the Crockett State Park). Built when I was eight or nine years old, it was the most impressive structure in town—a huge, shadowy palace with large ovals along the walls concealing indirect purple lighting, muted and surreal. There was a large curtain drawn across the giant screen, enhancing the anticipation as to what lay behind it. It was a place of wonder, a spark to any imagination, and the home of heroes where good and evil were unambiguous.

Good guys looked and dressed the part, were strong, brave, took up for the little guy, won against all odds, and apparently never had to make a living. Any little boy who didn't want to grow up to be like Roy Rogers or Gene Autry would have been cause for serious concern by his parents. At twenty cents to get in and a nickel for popcorn, it was the ultimate entertainment for me until I was grown. There, I lived in a state of suspended disbelief for as long as I possibly could, knowing that what was playing out on the screen before me was make-believe but resisting the acceptance of that fact until I absolutely had to go home. I wanted it to be real. Tarzan, the cavalry, and the occasional adult adventure that I would see with my parents took me to places I wanted to go to and usually made me feel good about myself. The impact that these radio-singers-turned-cowboy-actors made on me was profound.

Many years later, when I was in the United States Senate and attending a hearing, we were talking about how violence in the movies and television had increased over the years. I made a passing reference to growing up with Gene and Roy and watching them shoot a lot of bad guys. Soon I received a long letter from a Gene Autry–related organization taking umbrage and expressing outrage over my statement. They pointed out that Gene always shot the gun at the bad guy's hand. He never actually shot anybody. I stood corrected.

In those days, movies were perhaps the most significant common denominator in American society. If you walked into a bank almost anywhere in America, there was one thing you could almost always count on that would be shared by the bank president and the custodian: They grew up watching the same movies. At least for a while in our society, it helped to promote social cohesion—a common understanding as to what was just and unjust, good and evil. We all had the same examples of heroism and villainy.

I know it's probably hard to believe, but as a preteen in Lawrenceburg I was not exactly focused on the social significance of the cinema; I just wanted to go see "the show." But mind you, it had to be the right kind of movie. In other words, for my buddies and me it had to meet certain standards. It had to involve either guns, horses, or a jungle. It never occurred to us that our movie heroes were "actors" (nor to a lot of movie critics, I'll bet). Acting was for sissies. No self-respecting guy who wanted the approval of his peers would be caught dead onstage in a school play with a bunch of girls. Decidedly uncool. It was much better to sit back and make fun of the guys who did.

Each of us expressed our strength and independence by doing and thinking exactly as our buddies did. I broke from the pack only once—when I let a teacher talk me into playing Joseph in a Christmas play. I stood in one place with my trusty staff, sweating like a horse under heavy garb and a scratchy beard, for the entire duration of the play. I had no lines, of course. And I had to do rehearsals for that! After that experience, I returned to the herd and kept my record clean from there on out. Movies were fun, but "playacting" was not an appropriate activity for a real man. In fact, this finely honed sense of what was and was not acceptable in the area of movie fandom led me to an act of retribution that would make the Taliban proud.

It seems that all it takes to bring out a streak of meanness in an otherwise pretty good kid is a little encouragement and the opportunity to feel powerful and superior, even if it's for the briefest of times. If he is in fact a "pretty good kid," he'll feel guilty about it even half a century later. Thus, my episode with my next-door neighbor, Johnny.

I should have known that it would end in no good. The potential for violence was just too great. I was developing a powerful, if not lethal, right cross. It was a perfect complement to my left jab, which could cut a man's face to ribbons. I was developing into a boxing machine. I knew all of this because of the punishment I was doling out to an old Navy duffel bag filled with sawdust. Dad, remember, had wanted to be a boxer when he was a kid. I watched the Friday-night fights with him on TV and listened on a crackling radio when the likes of Rocky Marciano and Jake LaMotta fought for championships. He subscribed to *Ring Magazine,* and I would take old ones and cut out pictures of the fighters in action and stage my own fights on the kitchen table. I begged Dad for a set of boxing gloves, and sure enough, one Christmas under the tree I found two sets of boxing gloves and the homemade "heavy boxing bag."

After working on the bag enough to persuade myself that I was on my way to the big time, some of my buddies and I formed a "boxing club" in my garage, where I hung the bag and made space for a boxing "ring." However, I had a problem—a pretty basic one. These boxing skills that I was developing in my own mind were encased in a rather pudgy, slow, eleven-year-old body. I never fully appreciated the significance of the fact that the punching bag was stationary and didn't hit back. When inviting kids over to box, I didn't take the precaution of making sure that they were slower and fatter than I was. After a few jabs and fancy footwork, our sessions would turn into wild swinging melees in which we would occasionally connect with each other's head. It wasn't at all like it was on TV. And it could hurt like the dickens.

Nevertheless, we were all full of . . . whatever the precursor to testosterone is and still enjoyed mauling one another from time to time. All of which leads up to my neighbor Johnny. No, we didn't beat up Johnny. It's just that while we were perfecting our manly art, with decidedly mixed results, I became more and more resentful of the activity that was going on next door. Johnny had started a "movie star club," for Pete's sake! Johnny never had been on solid ground with me. I guess he was a nice enough guy, a skinny, pimply-faced kid like most of the rest of us. But his dad held a position that was well known to all of us kids—a position of prestige that caused us to be envious of Johnny. Even worse, Johnny was not hesitant to brag about it. His dad took the tickets at the door at the Crockett Theater.

I assumed that this meant Johnny had total access to all the movies. Even worse, he probably knew a lot of the movie stars. There were hints that drove us nuts. To us he was clearly using insider influence to get the pictures of the stars that he flaunted on the walls of his clubhouse, which was basically a little open shed in his backyard. To me his was a very sissy enterprise, at best. I was crazy about the cowboy and war movies, but none of the heroes from those films were on his wall. He actually had a lot of pictures of girls hanging up there. He even had girls in his club! What a dweeb, I thought. There was only one thing a macho, red-blooded, courageous boy could do—sneak over there in the dead of night, while nobody was looking, and tear the place up—which is what a buddy and I did. We tore some of the pictures in half (I didn't know at the time you could get them in magazines), turned over the crates they used for chairs, and mixed things around.

Of course, I began to feel bad as soon as my buddy went home—a confusing mix of conscience and a real fear of retribution from my folks. I was still hiding under the covers the next morning when I heard howls of anguish coming from across the yard. But that dreaded knock on my door never came. I assumed they had no idea who would do such a thing. Naturally, having gotten away with it, I felt even worse.

I think my little "Lord of the Flies" episode had a lasting effect on me. As an older kid and as an adult, I've had little tolerance for bullies either in the school yard or in my law practice. Nothing has given me more satisfaction than to be big enough or, as a lawyer, to have the ability to step up on occasion for the little guy who was being picked on by a governor or a state attorney general, for example. In all likelihood, I've been trying to make up for what I did to Johnny.

Also, I didn't miss the irony when my picture appeared many years later in a movie magazine that published an article about a movie I was in. I could envision somewhere a middle-aged Johnny ripping it to shreds.

All I can say to Johnny and my buddies back in school is, guys, if you're reading this, I really didn't mean to. I didn't mean to be an actor or be in the movies. It just kind of happened with no planning on my part. You know, just like it used to be with me growing up. How did it happen? Well, I've asked myself that question more than once—like the time I was in Durango, Mexico, many years after the incident with Johnny.

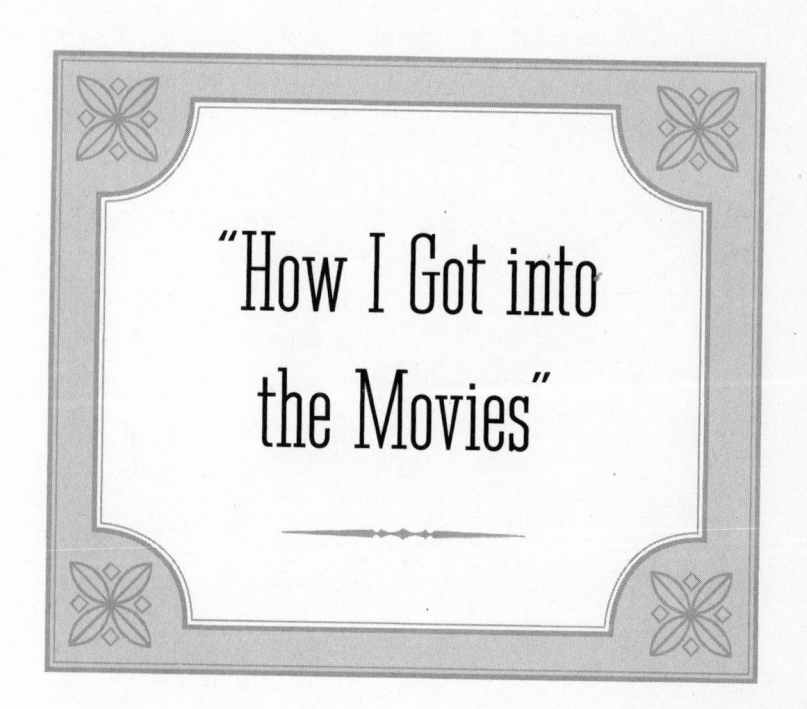

"How I Got into the Movies"

I HAD FORGOTTEN how hard it was to handle those big truck tires. Man, they were heavy. We hadn't had to deal with many of those around Dad's car lot, although I had made the acquaintance of a few during informal "strong boy" competitions at the Gulf Service Station on Cyclone Corner—Lawrenceburg's main intersection.

I had picked an unlikely place to become reunited with one of these babies. My tire and I were standing and waiting in an improvised hallway. The walls extended up only about eight feet. Above that was a makeshift roof at about twelve feet, leaving a gap of about four feet for the cold wind to blow through. It was 1988, and I was in the countryside outside of Durango, Mexico. If you were to see it, you could imagine a locale hospitable to drug traffickers or those coyotes who smuggle people over the border to the United States. But there I was, and feeling a good deal of pressure, although no drug deal was involved. That said, I couldn't help asking myself, "Is this an appropriate place for a re-spected barrister to be?"

On cue I straightened the coat of my military uniform and rolled my truck tire down the hallway, bursting through the double doors at the other end. Sitting behind a desk, also in a military uniform and looking shocked, was legendary actor Paul Newman. It was the first take of our scene to-gether on the set of *Fat Man and Little Boy,* the story of the making of the atomic bomb at Los Alamos, New Mexico, in the 1940s. Warner Brothers had re-created Los Alamos there on the barren Mexican landscape. Paul Newman and I were both playing U.S. Army generals. I played his boss, but for some reason Newman had the lead role.

I had already learned a valuable Hollywood lesson during the casting of this movie. The lead character in the real-life drama of making the A-bomb was a man by the name of Leslie Groves. He would also be the main character in the movie. The casting director had called my agent and de-scribed Groves as a large man, balding, who smoked cigars. They thought I might be just right for the part. They wanted to cast someone who actually looked like Groves. I felt the part fit me to a tee and was looking forward to my first lead-ing role. After a while, the casting director called back and said that although they wanted me to play another part in the movie, the part of Leslie Groves had gone to another actor. My agent asked who had gotten the part. The answer was

Paul Newman. The moral of that story was that if you can get Paul Newman, you get Paul Newman—presumably even if the part calls for the wearing of high heels and a hula skirt.

So I crashed my big truck tire through the double doors. The script called for me to be very angry and yelling loudly. I proceeded to berate Paul Newman while he sat there and looked at me with those famous baby blues. I had to concentrate like the devil to keep from thinking, "Geez, this is Paul Newman. I am cussing out Paul Newman."

Actually, the thought that did penetrate my consciousness was "How the devil did I wind up here?" The answer? In a quintessentially American way . . . I filed a lawsuit.

My client was a young woman by the name of Marie Ragghianti. While practicing law, I had seen many takeoffs on the theme of a woman done wrong by a man, but this one was going to be very different. The man was the governor of Tennessee, my old "friend" Ray Blanton, who had trounced my candidate, John T. Williams, when I made my political debut as Williams's campaign manager in 1968, one year out of law school. Blanton was also the guy Howard Baker beat in 1972 when I was Baker's campaign manager for Middle Tennessee. So I was one-and-one against "Sugar Ray" and felt that I knew him pretty well.

Before getting elected governor he had been a nondescript, hard-drinking rural congressman. He was said to be able to pick up a young pig by the ears and tell you exactly how old the pig was. Naturally, it was thought, a fellow like that ought to be in Congress. Lately, my main gripe against him was that he and his buddies were giving rednecks a bad name with their "country boys coming to town" shenanigans since they had taken over the governor's office. As it turned out, I had underestimated him.

Marie had spent a good part of 1973 in a sickbed recuperating from an illness. She had watched all of the Watergate hearings and took note of the young lawyer with the sideburns and funny suits and the fact that he was a fellow Tennessean. She thought to herself that if she ever needed a lawyer, this might be a good guy to have on her side. In June of 1978, when she walked into my office, that day had come. A few months before, she had been appointed by Ray Blanton to be chairman of the Pardons and Parole Board of Tennessee. A loyal Democrat, she had worked on his election bid and had become friends with a couple of his campaign people. However, when she called to make the appointment to see me, I vaguely recalled that the media had indicated that she had had a falling-out with the governor recently over her job performance. There turned out to be a lot more to it than that. She told me that the governor's legal counsel and others in the governor's office had become increasingly involved in the operation of the board. They would make "recommendations" as to who should be paroled from prison. They also wanted favorable recommendations from the board for pardons that the governor wanted to dole out. And the other board members were going along with the administration regardless of the merits of the individual cases. What's more, the governor's boys were applying pressure on behalf of some very unlikely jailbirds.

Soon after Marie became chairperson, she learned that the governor's legal counsel had scheduled a clemency hearing for an inmate by the name of Rose Lee Cooper because "her children needed her." Rose by any other name would still be a bad girl. Blanton had never exactly been known for his racial sensitivity, having supported George Wallace for president, but here we had a black, intercity woman from Memphis who had a long history of drug dealing and prostitution. The local district attorney had told Marie that Rose had national drug connections. As the probation report delicately put it when Rose was arrested, she was concealing cocaine "between her legs." Not a likely candidate for clemency, one might think. Marie voted against her, and the other two board members nervously followed Marie's lead. It was the first time the governor's office had ever been rejected.

After a few similar episodes, it got to the point that the governor was clearly looking for a reason to fire Marie. She wanted my advice. I had to take off my political hat and put on my counselor's hat (as much as it pained me). She told me that she needed the job and that she was the sole support for her three children. I advised her that unless she had specific evidence of wrongdoing, she was probably better off trying to simply go on doing the best job she could and hoping for the best. Maybe the risk of bad press would deter them, I suggested. Besides, under Tennessee law the board members served at the governor's pleasure and he could fire her for "good cause," and good cause had been interpreted to be almost anything that the governor determined it to be.

Within a few days, she was back in my office. It had all hit the fan. The state auditor had carried out a secret audit of Marie's travel and expense records and found discrepancies. The governor issued a press release and a copy of a letter he was sending to Marie firing her and essentially accusing her of fraudulent conduct. It was all over the newspapers and television. "Well," I figured, "Marie has finally given them the bullets to shoot her with."

Instead of being intimidated, Marie was fit to be tied. She wanted to sue the governor for wrongful termination. Marie's secretary, a loyal administration employee, had filled out the expense sheets for her, and even using the governor's figures, the discrepancies amounted to a grand total of $59.05 in overcharges to the state. The amount, of course, was not mentioned in the press. Marie sneaked out a copy of her own records, and as we went over them in my office, it was obvious that what we were looking at was a penny-ante hatchet job on Marie.

Still, I tried to talk her out of a lawsuit. They could make her life miserable in ways that she could not understand. It was best that she get on with her life, et cetera, et cetera. I figured that the governor's office was undoubtedly applying pressure on the board for political reasons; that was wrong, maybe scandalous, but probably not illegal. On top of that, Marie had uttered the most terrifying words that a lawyer can ever hear: "I am broke." Still, she was adamant. "What about a contingency fee?" she asked.

"One-third of nothing is not much of a fee," I replied.

"There is no way that a jury would side with them on this," she countered.

"We probably can't get a jury trial," I added. Back and forth we went.

The more I thought about it, the more I knew she was right about one thing: What they had done to her was cruel and unfair. The governor's letter was designed not just to fire her but to punish her. From all I could learn, Marie had been extremely conscientious, working overtime to upgrade a parole board that sorely needed it. She was adamant that the law be followed and cases be decided on their merits. For that, the governor had impugned her integrity and tried to humiliate her for his own nefarious reasons, whatever they were. I could see the theme of a trial emerging: "The governor didn't fire this woman because she was not doing her job. He fired her because she *was* doing her job." Sounded pretty good. What the heck. I wasn't that busy, and I never did like

Blanton anyway. It would be fun to rattle his cage. So I took the case on a contingency, and we did manage to get the judge to give us a jury trial. Now we were playing in our ballpark.

Unbeknownst to us, the FBI had put this information together with other leads they had in their possession, resulting in a very troubling picture of potential widespread corruption in the Blanton administration. Before long, Marie was working with them closely. It seems that our civil trial for wrongful termination was going to be the tip of a very large iceberg. Although the proof was still developing and Marie and I were limited to the facts of our case, we were able to paint enough of a picture of what was going on in Tennessee's criminal justice system that the truth became apparent during our trial. She had been the only impediment to putting rapists and murderers back on the street after serving absurdly short periods of time in jail. Much to everyone's surprise (including my own), we won our case, even though one of our key witnesses had been mysteriously murdered days before the trial.

The verdict was front-page news across the state, with all the details of all the suspicious circumstances, and soon people began to come forward with additional information. Then the FBI developed an informant, and after that they carried out a sting operation. The governor's house of cards came tumbling down. His legal counsel and his assistant had been selling pardons and paroles out of the governor's office. They were convicted and sent to prison. Ray Blanton was convicted of selling a liquor license.

A few months after our trial, I received another call from Marie. She wanted to know if I wanted to go with her to listen to a talk that was being given by Peter Maas, the famous author of many books, including *Serpico, The Valachi Papers,* and *The King of the Gypsies.* He was appearing at a function in Nashville, and she wanted to tell him her story. I probably rolled my eyes while politely declining. The next day, she called me again. She said that she had met Peter Maas; that they had had a long talk, she told him the Blanton story, and she thought he might be interested in writing something about it.

I assumed the role of the wise and worldly older brother and explained that probably what Peter was interested in was her and that she shouldn't allow him to lead her on. After all, a governor going to jail was not that big of a story. A week or so later, she called me back. "Peter is still interested in doing something with our story," she said.

Losing patience, I said, "If he is interested in this story, have him come to see me and explain why one of the best-known writers of nonfiction in America thinks that this Tennessee tale is worthy of his time."

A few days later, lo and behold, with Marie in tow, Peter Maas, a sporty gentleman with a shock of gray hair and dark bushy eyebrows, was sitting across from me in my office, chain-smoking dark cigarillos, and answering my questions. "It's not a political story, it's a personal story—a courageous woman's story. This battered divorcée, sole support of her three children, working at everything from a cocktail waitress to volunteering at the Catholic church, putting herself through Vanderbilt University, who had the best job that she'd ever had—this woman put it all on the line (the only one to do so) in order to stand up for the right thing. And this, by the way, was while all of the men around her were cowering."

"Wow," I said. "Doggone it, I knew we had a story here." It was Marie's turn to roll her eyes.

I went to New York and negotiated the book deal with Sam Cohn of ICM, Peter's agent. The result was *Marie: A True Story,* published a year later, in which Peter followed the original vision he'd outlined in my office. The lead-up to our trial was the integral part of the story, with the trial itself written as the closing chapter. Marie and I were both pleased with the final product and marveled at the research that had gone into the book—the detail and drama that this consummate professional was able to weave together. And Marie deserved to have her story told. But the story was not quite over.

Of course, it never occurred to me at the time that just about everything Peter Maas had ever written was made into a movie or a television treatment. Sure enough, Dino De

Laurentiis, the legendary film producer, bought the rights to *Marie*. I was pleased, but I took no special note of it. I was back to building my law practice and making a living, which meant bringing in some cases more remunerative than Marie's had been.

Several weeks later, however, I found myself enjoying a pleasant change of pace reliving the Marie–Blanton saga over drinks and dinner with some new acquaintances. In Nashville, we were used to rubbing shoulders with country music stars (I had briefly represented Waylon Jennings, and I sued George Jones for another client), but we didn't get a lot of Hollywood traffic. But that night, I was having dinner with the producer, Frank Capra, Jr., and the director, Roger Donaldson. They were going to make the Marie movie and were talking with people who had had a part in the real-life drama in order to get the flavor of the story and to help them in supervising the writing of the script. I was one of many they were talking to, but we hit it off and over the next few months had periodic bull sessions. They told me that Debra Winger was considered for the role of Marie but that the part went to Sissy Spacek. They mentioned other potential cast members, including someone who was going to have a small role as one of the other board members, a little-known actor by the name of Morgan Freeman. Part of the movie would be shot in Nashville. Some Nashvillians would probably be used for "walk-on" parts, and they told me they would put me on the list. That was fine with me; I thought it would give me a chance to see how a movie was made.

One day a few weeks later, I was in the office when Roger Donaldson called. They were going to have a casting call at the Sheraton Hotel across the street from my office and asked if I would be interested in coming over and reading something for them. He said he would send it over in advance. "Sure," I said, "we can catch up." As I hung up, I could envision a scene where I would walk in and say something like, "Your car is waiting, ma'am," and on opening night my friends and I could laugh about it.

The line of people waiting to get into the Sheraton for auditions for the walk-ons and extras went around the block. In fact, my daughter Betsy, then twenty-one, and my long-time assistant, Bobbie Murphy, were in the line, and both became extras. My movie-mogul friends had already arranged for me to come in a side door to save me the embarrassment from appearing to do exactly what I was doing. I wasn't above being one of the mob clamoring to get a bit part in a movie, but I *was* above anybody knowing that I was doing it. A professional man has got an image to keep up. The guys back in Lawrenceburg would certainly not have approved of me sneaking in a side door to get a bit part in a movie.

A couple of hours before I went over to the Sheraton, a few pages that looked like part of a movie script arrived. It was a scene with Marie Ragghianti and "Fred." Being quick on the uptake, I concluded that that would be *me*. Whoa, this was getting interesting. It had never occurred to me that my character would have a part in the movie. I assumed that for courtroom scenes they would use fictionalized versions of the characters other than Marie.

I went over and was taken to a hotel room with a small motion-picture camera on a tripod in the corner of the room. I told Roger, "Hey, I don't do porn movies unless the pay is right." "You wish," Roger replied. Roger introduced me to the only other person in the room, Lynn Stalmaster, who I later learned was one of the leading casting directors in Hollywood. I sat down in front of the camera, and Lynn stood behind it and read Marie's part as we did the scene (with me looking down at the script as needed). When we finished, Stalmaster said, "Not bad," and walked out.

I asked Roger what was going on. He told me that my character was in several scenes in the movie, including the trial, the lead-up to the trial, and noncourtroom stuff such as the scene we had just read. Several guys screen-tested for my role, but the producers weren't satisfied. They decided to give me a shot at it if I was interested. Things were moving from interesting to a little bizarre.

Back in my office, I had to laugh at the thought of it. It occurred to me that if I was going to play myself, they couldn't tell me that I was doing it wrong (an incorrect assumption, I later learned). I refused to let myself take it seriously. I didn't know much about show business, but I knew enough to know that they didn't walk up to a guy who had never been in so much as a high school play and say, "How would you like to play yourself in a movie?" Besides, what about my schedule? I probably couldn't do it if I wanted to. On the other hand, if it did happen, wouldn't it be a kick. Maybe I could act. Some might say I had been doing it for several years. Then I would snap out of it, and it would be "Thompson, quit being an idiot. Get back to work on that brief."

It was more than a month before Roger called again. I had long since relegated the matter to the back of my mind. "Mr. De Laurentiis wants to know if you could come to New York and read another scene for us." My first reaction was to tell him that I couldn't possibly make it before eight o'clock the next morning, but that might have appeared to be overly eager.

A few days later I was in New York before the camera again, except there were several more people present. It was apparent that they were not all there for me. Actors were all over the place auditioning for minor roles. De Laurentiis didn't attend this session. He watched the film later. Many months later, I was told that when he first saw me on the screen, he pointed and exclaimed in a heavy Italian accent, "Blan-ton, Blan-ton." He apparently thought I would be perfect for the role of Ray Blanton. "No, Fred Thompson,"

Roger told him. "No, Blan-ton," De Laurentiis insisted. "No, that really is Fred Thompson," Roger tried to explain. Roger finally persuaded him that it would not be a good idea for me to play Ray Blanton.

Before long, Frank Capra was in my office again. They wanted me to take the part—to play myself in the movie. By then I had read the script and knew that it would be a sizable role. Wow. By the time of the meeting, I was definitely up for taking on this new challenge if it came my way. It was a door I wanted to walk through. In weighing the situation, it seemed to me that it presented a disadvantage and an advantage. The disadvantage was not knowing what the heck I was doing. The advantage was that by not being an actor, and by being totally out of my element, if I fell on my face it would not be that big a deal. I'd never had an acting lesson (later a buddy told me that for those who had seen my work, it wasn't necessary for me to point this out anymore). Anyway, Frank got down to business and asked me if I had an agent. "Of course not," I replied, but I was a lawyer and had in fact negotiated the original Marie book deal. Then I proceeded to prove that a lawyer who represents himself has a fool for a client. Capra said we needed to talk about money. I think I stopped myself barely in time—because my first thought was "I wonder how much he expects me to pay them?" I let him talk long enough for me to see that they were going to pay me an amount I considered to be a fair fee for this lark. Besides, what difference did the amount make?

This was a one-time deal. It wasn't like the amount was going to set a precedent that other filmmakers could use against me in the future when I might want more money. R–i–i–g–h–t.

Of course, this turned out to be the first of twenty feature-film roles for me, as well as numerous television roles and commercials. The decision to take one of the least remunerative and longest-shot cases I'd ever had led to one of the most interesting chapters of my life. It's like I opened the door to what I thought was the courthouse and walked into Disneyland.

Maybe it wasn't so outlandish for me to think I could play different characters. After all, I'd grown up with a pretty rich assortment of them in Lawrenceburg, starting with my own family. And speaking of family, parents should be mindful that when they tell a kid he or she can do anything they set their mind to, as I was told. The kid might just believe it, whether the parent does or not. So tell them. This was very much on my mind a few years ago when they had a little ceremony for me in Lawrenceburg and had me leave my autograph and foot- and handprints in wet cement in front of the old Crockett Theater, where I had spent so much time in my youth. (One old-timer said he wasn't surprised to learn that my feet were in concrete but he never thought it would be for an occasion such as this.)

In an additional irony, it was my brother Ken, eight years

younger, who turned out to be the real actor. Well trained, he has appeared on stage in numerous professional productions. Most remarkable of all, after I told him I was going to be in the movies and his knowing that previously I had no interest or preparation, he was still speaking to me.

But anyway, Johnny, I'm terribly sorry about that movie star club thing.

Rebel Motors

DURING MY EIGHTH-GRADE YEAR, we moved to Nashville. Dad wanted to try his hand at selling cars for a dealership in the big city. We rented the smallest house in a nice neighborhood, close to a church Mom and Dad had selected. I enrolled at the Glendale Public School, one of the best in the area. The governor's son and a bank president's sons were in my class. I was undoubtedly the only kid in the eighth grade who didn't have a suit or know how to dance. I most definitely did not make up for my deficiencies with academic achievement. They were studying a different kind of math. Of course, for me any kind of math would have been different—ever since I learned my multiplication tables, I sort of rested on my laurels—but out of embarrassment I struggled and tried harder. Dad said to me, "I told you, son, if you want any help from me you are going to have to stay in the seventh grade." As usual, Dad's humor contained an element of truth.

To top off the year, I couldn't make the softball team and got turned down when I finally mustered up the courage to ask a girl out on what would have been my first date. Other than that, it was a great year. Actually, it didn't work out too well for any of us. Dad, whose business had always depended on his personal relationships built over many years, was pretty much of a lost ball in the high weeds in the Nashville car market. And my little brother, Ken, came down with rheumatic fever. If all of this seems like the makings of a bad country song, it seemed that way to us, too. As for me, something clearly drastic had to be done. I was going to have to either really buckle down and shape up or leave town. Thankfully, we left town. We moved back to Lawrenceburg. Mom had to clean up two new houses within one year. But Lawrenceburg never looked so good.

Back in Lawrenceburg, what with my big-city experience and greater understanding of the ways of the world, I was upgraded to a more responsible position. I got to clean up old cars at Dad's lot, which he'd moved up the road on Highway 43 North, toward Nashville. He took an old bus, put it on a concrete foundation, and made it into an office at the back of a 150-foot by 150-foot lot, which was big enough to hold twenty cars or so. This time, Dad went into partnership with his brother, Mitch, who was three years younger than Dad, with movie-star looks and dark wavy hair. Having inherited the Thompson gene of avoidance of salaried employment and guaranteed paychecks, he too chose to become a "car man"—and was a good one. Quick with a joke and a laugh, he was what could euphemistically be called a "free spirit." After his divorce he "ran pretty hard" for a few years, with more than a passing familiarity with women, drink, and automobile wrecks—sometimes all at once. More than once he was in the wrong place at the wrong time. One night the police shot through the windshield of his car, mistaking him for a handsome outlaw famous in Tennessee at the time. At least, that was Mitch's story.

Some of my earliest memories are of Dad and Mitch sitting around after dinner laughing and talking about their exploits while growing up. Mitch's personality, even as a kid, was aptly demonstrated by a story Dad used to love to tell. One day a young Mitch was teasing some old man who was about out of it. Dad chastised him: "Mitch, cut it out. That old man is almost ninety years old." "I don't care," Mitch said, grinning. "I could whip him if he was a hundred." Dad saved his hide more than once. He dearly loved Mitch even as their personal lives as adults took different paths. Mom liked Mitch, but needless to say she was not impressed by some of his habits and exploits, even though he eventually settled down. But one thing everybody agreed on: Mitchell Thompson paid his debts. In Lawrenceburg, if you paid your debts, folks would cut you some slack. Even your sister-in-law.

They had a third partner—a fellow by the name of Half Durrett, an old friend of the family. They named their place

Rebel Motors and had a grand opening with balloons and banners. When the local radio guy from WDXE came by to sell them some advertising time, Mitch had a great idea for a radio commercial: "Don't Be a Son of a B———, Trade with Half, Fletch, and Mitch." That provided laughs for several days before an ad that was a little more conventional was settled on.

I think that Tennessee in August was the time and place the phrase "It's not the heat, it's the humidity" was born. With my shirt off, and with sweat pouring off of me like water, I'd clean up the cars on the lot that had been bought or traded for. Then, after sweeping them out, I'd spray down the cars with a hose and wash them. Then I would go inside the "office," stand in front of the air conditioner, and listen to a little country music and the deep and complex existential messages that the songs conveyed. There was the Everly Brothers' drive-in-movie classic lyrics "Wake up, Little Susie, wake up . . . We fell asleep, our goose is cooked, our reputation is shot," or Webb Pierce singing, "You say that you loved me, but I know it's a lie, so tell me why, baby, why." How could a fellow listen to that and not have a deeper understanding of life?

I can still remember the lyrics to dozens of those songs (learned while other kids wasted their time on things like algebra)—possibly because I heard them so often, but maybe because the theme was usually about hard living, drinking, and boy-girl stuff, none of which I had had any experience with but which seemed to permeate the atmosphere of my little Southern town in the 1950s. Someone once said that the perfect country song would be something like this: "I lost my job and was drinking the day my mama got out of prison, 'cause my woman just left me when my car broke down after I had run over her best dog. Then my luck turned bad."

I liked working at the car lot. The pay wasn't much and the work was uninspiring, but you couldn't beat the cultural side benefits.

It was a banner day for me when Half took in an old motorbike as part of a trade-in. The contraption looked like someone literally had taken an old bicycle and put a motor and rigging on it, but to me it gleamed like a new Harley-Davidson. I annoyed Half about it—very subtly, of course—until finally he just gave it to me. I was shocked; Half was going to be out $10 or $15, I thought. There was a little problem with my cycle: It had no brakes. I don't mean that it had bad brakes or brakes in need of repair: It had *no* brakes.

I did not see this as a problem. Brakes were a luxury I saw no particular need for. I would simply learn to anticipate when I was going to need to slow down (a talent I could have used later in life). When I came to a traffic light, for instance, I figured I would let up on the gas, and when I slowed down enough, I'd just drag my feet until I stopped. Miraculously, with no license, no helmet, and obviously no clue, I rode that motorcycle without incident for about a year. What got me off the bike wasn't a run-in with the law or another inanimate object, like a wall; it was a few of my slightly older buddies and an occasional girl whizzing by me in their cars, laughing. It occurred to me that I was not being looked upon as especially cool. This, of course, could not be tolerated.

Although I had been around them all my life, I was never interested in cars the way many of my buddies were. I was never a gearhead; I always looked at them as something to get you someplace, without a lot of romance connected with it. Dad never taught me anything about them, and I never really asked. I figured later that he probably thought he was doing me a favor and he probably had other things on his mind. Observing him on the lot doing business was interesting. There was no fancy filing system inside that bus on the blocks of an office, no computerized inventory. Dad was able to keep track in his head of what he had "in" a car, and often that car was on the lot as the result of several other trades. He had to know the answer in order to calculate his profit when he priced the car for sale.

Amid the jokes and the occasional flurry of activity, life on the lot for me was mostly unrelenting monotony with long stretches of absolutely nothing to do. For all of his outgoing personality, Dad could be very quiet and self-contained. He would walk the lot or look out the window, lost in his own thoughts, seemingly almost sad. Dad was an interesting guy in a lot of ways. His handwriting was beautiful. Also, after I was grown, Ma Thompson showed me a picture that Dad had drawn as a young boy. It was a drawing of cowboys sitting around a campfire, and it looked almost professional. I hadn't known that he could draw. In addition, he had a beautiful bass voice and sang not only in church but in informal quartets at funerals. I sometimes wondered what he was thinking about, although it never occurred to me to ask because I knew it would never have occurred to him to answer. I assumed it was part of being an adult. My opinion hasn't changed much about that. What I was witnessing, of course, was just a man making a living. Possibly hardwired to be a little melancholy, he was playing out an age-old process. Doing the only thing he knew, without the benefit of a formal education or assistance from family or government; without a pension plan or health insurance, knowing that his family depended on prospective customers deciding to pull off of Highway 43 onto his car lot and what kind of mood they were in. But he knew that he was better off than his parents had been and that almost everybody he knew was pretty much in the same boat. And at least he always had a chance at having a really good year, as he judged it. He had some of those good years, and I never heard him express any misgivings, doubts, or regrets about anything.

As for me, I didn't like the feel of this glimpse into the world of earning a living. I am sure it probably showed in my work habits. I am just as sure that Dad would have been surprised to know that about forty years later, down the road on

Highway 43 within sight of his lot, there would be a sign that read "Welcome to Lawrenceburg, Tennessee, Home of Fred Thompson."

But it's funny how so often life comes full circle. In politics they say that sincerity is very important. Once you are able to fake that, the rest of it is easy. But even more important than sincerity is authenticity, and authenticity can't be faked. Over thirty-five years after my car-lot days, I decided to run for the U.S. Senate. I had never run for public office before, and I knew that I would be going up against a fourteen-year veteran of the House of Representatives—a Rhodes scholar whose father had been governor of Tennessee. He also would have a good head start on me in fundraising. Nevertheless, I had simply become fed up with standing on the sidelines complaining about the government, and I decided it was time to put up or shut up. Of course, being a political neophyte, it turned out to be harder than I thought it would be. For several months I was getting nowhere and lagging in the polls. My campaign had rented a fancy van with all the latest equipment and put me in the back of it in a suit and tie as we traveled from stop to stop. It wasn't fun.

One day I was having lunch with an old friend of mine, Tom Ingram, who had helped another friend, Lamar Alexander, get elected governor of Tennessee. I had left the campaign trail for a couple of hours, and we were chowing down at a Cracker Barrel restaurant. I was complaining about my circumstances and finally said, "You know, if it was left up to me, I would just get in an old pickup truck and drive across the state, stopping whenever I wanted to talk to people." Tom replied something to the effect of "Then why don't you do it? That's who you are." "Yeah," I thought. "That is who I am." Back at the campaign the opinion was unanimous. Bad idea. So we did it anyway.

We found a red 1990 Chevrolet "straight stick" Silverado, and with a staff guy to drive me, we took off and did exactly what I envisioned. Wearing my jeans and boots, we would pull up in the middle of a crowd at a campaign stop and I would hop into the back of the truck bed and give 'em hell. It all fit. I was having fun, and folks said that it was showing. As I started climbing in the polls, my opposition unloaded on me. "He is a fraud," they said. "He's not really a good ole boy, but a champagne-sipping, Gucci-wearing, Grey Poupon–spreading Washington insider." Frankly, I thought that was the best line of the campaign. But I also thought that accusing me of sipping champagne in Jack Daniel's country was over the line. I replied that my opponent was just jealous that he didn't have the advantages that I had by my *not* being a Rhodes scholar. I knew that I had 'em. I knew that I was coming off as exactly who I was.

The truck became pretty famous. We had campaign pins and buttons made with pictures of the truck on it. Sometimes when I would go out of state, folks would say, "Yeah, you're the fellow with the red truck." The old red pickup truck now resides at the Baker Center at the University of Tennessee, where I donated my papers.

My opponent didn't know about my dad, the car lot, and the way I grew up. When I had gotten into trouble with the campaign, I had simply gone back to my roots, including an old truck just like the ones I used to drive and clean up on my dad's lot.

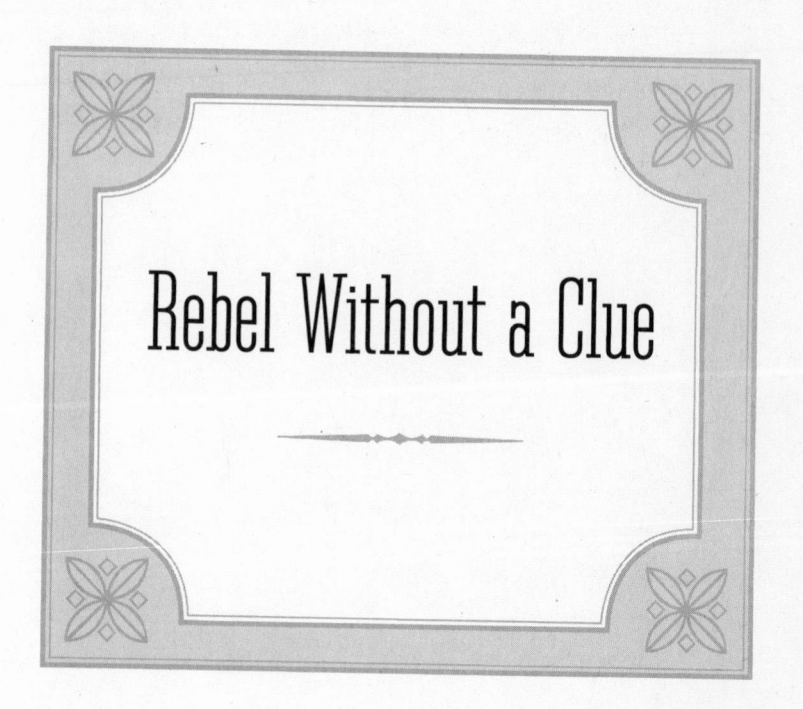

Rebel Without a Clue

Teaching Latin to someone like me in high school was somewhat like trying to teach a pig to dance. It's a waste of the teacher's time and it irritates the pig. But such was the task that Mrs. Garner accepted at Lawrence County High School—with predictable results. If there is such a thing as teacher's heaven where the saints of the profession go, then Mrs. Garner is undoubtedly there—for not having someone shoot me, or for not doing the deed herself. And there's not a jury in the state that would have convicted her.

Mrs. Garner was a heavyset, middle-aged lady of mild disposition. Even I didn't know how steady her temperament was until that day she walked into class—as usual, exactly at the time for the class to start—and took her seat at her desk. I, along with another classmate with no visible signs of redemption, had come into possession of a small supply of "cracker balls," which were very popular around the Fourth of July and Christmas season. They were like little round firecrackers, not much bigger than a large pea, and when you threw them on the sidewalk they made a pretty loud pop. Before class that day we put a cracker ball under each of the four legs of Mrs. Garner's chair. She came in, sat down, and two or three of them went off. In the classroom it sounded like gunfire. Then something remarkable happened—nothing. Without so much as flinching, she proceeded to scoot her chair in behind her desk and begin the class as if nothing had happened. Man, this was awe-inspiring. And with that she managed to cause me to experience the one emotion that I hated most—shame. To my mind, her forbearance was even more remarkable in light of the fact that the chances of her being able to finger the right culprits in that class were about 99.9 percent. She wouldn't even have had to "round up the usual suspects." They were sitting right there in front of her, trying their best to look shocked and surprised. But she didn't. I was so impressed, I even made a halfhearted attempt to learn a few Latin words, and I did. I just never learned what they meant.

Attempting to create "shock and awe" in class was not the only "independent study" I undertook to endear myself to the faculty. Every day we had to put in an hour in study hall. It was a large auditorium full of desks. My challenge every day was to decide how best to kill the time in study hall. Given that farming is a major part of life in Tennessee, we had a teacher who taught agriculture and was also our study hall teacher my sophomore year. Mr. Ag was a big, raw-boned fellow with straight blond hair. He could have posed for a Norman Rockwell painting. He was also what we called "wall-eyed." His eyes just didn't go in the same direction at the same time. When one was looking northeast, the other one was looking southwest. You can imagine the sensitivity my buddies and I demonstrated in our discussions about his appearance.

As best I could tell, he had two jobs in his role as study hall monitor as he sat on a slightly elevated platform and looked out over the auditorium. First, he had to evaluate the sneezes. Practically every day, once or twice, someone would let out a loud sneeze. Occasionally, one of them would be a real sneeze. Others were borderline, and most often they would be accompanied by a rhetorical flourish wherein the sneeze sounded like a dirty word. The teacher had to evaluate these sneezes as to whether or not they were fake or genuine and, if fake, dole out the appropriate punishment—usually demerits. But, of course, demerits didn't inflict pain, and with us, anything that didn't hurt did not serve as much of a deterrent. His second job was to be the restroom cop. People who wanted to go to the restroom had to sign a slip of paper and hand it to him on the way out.

Given Mr. Ag's appearance, he was naturally a target-rich environment for the artistically inclined. One day I decided to work on my portrait skills by drawing Mr. Ag's face. I was doing a pretty good job, if I do say so myself. I especially wanted to get the eyes just right. I was concentrating heavily on that, and just before I finished I felt the presence of someone standing to my left and slightly behind me. Much to my chagrin, I looked up to see my subject, Mr. Ag. He was looking (as best as I could tell) directly at my handiwork. "Not bad," he said, and walked on. Another close call. However, I knew better than to ask permission to go to the restroom for the rest of that semester during study hall, although I surely could have used a restroom break the moment I looked up and saw him standing there.

Yes, life for me in high school was pretty good. The only cloud on the horizon was provided by narrow-minded teachers who insisted that I show up on time and not talk in class. They bombarded me with demerits, which would be dutifully recorded by them on "pink cards," which became a part of my permanent record. Given my rate of production of pink cards, I could imagine a "Freddie Thompson" file cabinet drawer dedicated solely to me.

The school faculty continued to remind me that they would follow me and haunt me for the rest of my life, and, well, I couldn't have that. And my response? What I thought would be the response of any red-blooded American boy— eliminate the pink cards. One day during one of my frequent trips to the principal's office, where the pink cards were kept, I unlatched the window to the office, which was on the ground floor. I recruited another ne'er-do-well buddy, and we agreed that it would be a real hoot if we came over that night, sacked up all the pink cards, and took them to the woods and buried them to protect them from the prying eyes of future unknown busybodies intent upon ruining our glorious futures. Of course, school officials would have no idea who pulled off this brilliant caper. Never mind that I would probably rank as the top three suspects on any list. Or that when questioned I was the worst liar in the history of delinquency and usually I fessed up after the first question.

Nevertheless, the two of us laughed all the way to the school that night, enjoying the brilliance of our scheme. We continued to laugh when we discovered that the long horizontal window would open only halfway and we could not stuff our oversized bodies through it. And we were probably laughing with relief when we realized we weren't going to be able to pull off the pink-card theft. We figured we'd eluded the night watchman, done our best, and when trying to right an injustice, it's the thought that counts.

It didn't occur to me until years later that it was only a matter of a few inches that prevented me from committing a felony before even leaving high school. They say that God protects drunks and children. I would add young morons to that list.

One of my other pals had his dad's car one night, and a few of us were driving around when we saw this large sign,

"Gone Fishing," over a bait and tackle shop on the outskirts of town. It took a considerable amount of time for us to get that sign unhinged and transported over to the high school. But it was more than worth the effort when we gazed upon our handiwork after we had nailed the sign up above the entrance to the study hall, which could be seen from the rest of the campus. The sign was up so high that it actually took the maintenance people two or three days to get it down, giving us plenty of time to appreciate the results of our hard work.

It's not as though all my shenanigans went unpunished. In the arts and sometimes in sports, it is said that a person should be judged by their "body of work." Unfortunately, that's what happened to me. I was about to learn a valuable lesson. If you act like a jerk, the people you have offended will eventually get an opportunity to nail you—and often when it hurts the most.

In my junior year, I achieved what at the time seemed like the most important achievement in a person's life: recognition by high school classmates. The juniors, showing great insight, voted me the Most Athletic boy. I had officially arrived. In my own mind, in three years I was transformed from a slow-footed nonathletic little boy to a real "hoss." This analysis was now shared by the ultimate arbiter—my fellow classmates of Lawrence County High School.

However, unbeknownst to me, several of the teachers got together soon after the election and decided that—election or not—no one with my academic and deportment record should be allowed to be a Superlative at Lawrence County High School. They decreed that I should be stripped of my honor and a new election held. Even worse, the teachers were being led by Mrs. Eleanor Buckner, mother of one of my high school buddies. Of course, I was outraged. I wanted to know, "What does athletics have to do with school and good conduct, for Pete's sake?" With this kind of thinking I was ahead of my time. "What about the election? What about just making up new rules to get the results they want? Who do they think they are, the Supreme Court?" I would even have thrown in a "due process" argument if I had ever heard of it. However, it never occurred to me that I had any real recourse. Those were the days before students and their parents filed lawsuits against schools for violation of constitutional or other rights. Besides, I wanted to keep my parents out of it. They knew me better than anybody, and I knew they would be on the teachers' side. As Mom said, "If you had behaved yourself, this wouldn't have happened." I had to consider seriously whether behaving myself would have been worth it. A heavy price to pay, it seemed to me.

Ironically, it was a teacher who showed me mercy when I needed it the most. Mrs. Little was the mother of another one of my football teammates. Unfortunately for her, she was also my French teacher my senior year. Toward the end of the year, I began to realize that my grade situation was worse than I thought. In fact, I needed to pass French in order to graduate, and in order to get a passing grade, I had to pass my final French exam. There was only one problem. I hardly knew any French at all. Unlike Latin, French wasn't a dead language, but it might as well have been, as far as I was concerned. I did think that the French accent of some of those guys in the movies was pretty cool, but that was about the extent of my association with the language. To my great surprise, my survival instincts and natural adaptability failed me, and I failed my final French exam.

Now things were really getting serious. For the first time in my life, my sense of humor and well-honed "cool kid" nonchalance could do nothing for me. No clever response or prank could get me out of the hole I had dug for myself. The possibility of failing high school had never occurred to me. I had figured that getting a gentleman's C with no work made a lot more sense than an A or B with a lot of work. Unfortunately, an occasional D or F would rear its ugly head, obviously more times than I had realized. I was distraught.

One day, as the semester was drawing to a close, Mrs. Little asked to see me. She asked if she gave me my French test over again, or a test similar to it, did I think I could pass it. "Absolutely," I said. She gave me a couple of days to prepare, and I hit the books with a newfound sense of desperation. This was that second chance that the screwups are always saying they deserve. I knew that there wouldn't be a third chance. So I passed the test. I never knew why Mrs. Little reached out to me like that. She had never been especially friendly to me before. Maybe she saw some potential in me. Maybe she felt sorry for me. Or maybe, in fact most likely of all, she was dreading the prospect of having me in her class again the following year.

I was grateful for being given a second chance. But mostly I was relieved—that Mom and Dad would not have to face the shame of seeing their oldest boy fail to accomplish what for them would have been a first: having at least one of us graduate from high school. As with so many things in life, between children and parents, I never really knew how important my graduating from high school was to them until many years later, when my dad went back and earned his own high school equivalency certificate.

In the end, I managed to graduate from high school with barely enough credits. In our school annual that year, everyone was given a saying or a motto under their photograph. Under mine were the words "The less I do today, the more I plan to do tomorrow."

"Play Ball!" . . .
but Not Forever

WHAT CAUSES a man to dream about the one that got away in high school almost fifty years ago? You look back and right before you is the most beautiful thing you ever saw in your life. It just wasn't meant to be. You let what should have been slip right through your fingers. You'd give anything for another chance. This was not a girl. It was the most perfectly thrown football I had ever seen, and it was coming right at me as I stood in the end zone.

Sports metaphors and life lessons learned from sports could fill (and have filled) innumerable books. Usually they have to do with such things as the importance of teamwork and not being deterred by temporary setbacks. Retired sports celebrities receive large fees for reminding companies' employees that it takes an entire organization "working together" to build a good hedge-trimming machine.

For the true sports fan, the game need serve no higher

purpose than the game itself. And games need to be played. Every little boy knows instinctively that the ball needs to be thrown, kicked, or hit. Then the transition begins. Having been taught all our young lives to share and be mindful of the feelings of others, we are introduced to the joys of sticking it to our best friends. We graduate from the joyous mayhem of the backyard to the school yard to the adult-supervised contests. And we learn as we grow older that behind every potbellied know-it-all fan and every pencil-necked sportswriter probably lies a bittersweet tale of unrequited love. Once upon a time, if only for a little while, they too were the boys of summer. They were going to be able to run faster, grow bigger, and do all the things that their college and professional heroes did. Then they had their first experience with their dreams not working out.

For most kids who are moderately interested in sports, reality sets in at an early age. It's when Dad pitches them "batting practice" (underhanded) for the first time and after forty or so pitches there is no contact between bat and ball. Junior begins to get the picture, his interest with regard to that particular sport becomes somewhat aligned with his ability, and he moves on to other sports or other pursuits.

However, an intense interest in sports is hardwired into some kids. They may have a bit more ability than the average kid, but that really doesn't matter so much in terms of their passion. They choose their teams, worship their heroes, and most of all they want to play. They cling to the notion that someday they'll be good enough not only to play but to play out their fantasies, too.

Little League baseball is most boys' introduction to competitive, organized sports. It is here, among the team selections, intense drills and practices, and tension-filled games, that we learn the true meaning of "the thrill of victory and the agony of defeat."

Many timid young boys think that baseball would be a wonderful game if you didn't have to bat. Ironically, it was probably the greatest left-handed hitter of all time, Ted Williams, who gave voice to every little boy's anxiety who had to come in from right field and bat: "They give us a round bat to hit a round ball. And then tell us to hit it squarely." It's not that deep down I didn't want to bat, I just didn't care to display my skills in front of all those people watching, since my success rate in making contact with the ball was not very high. For me, the world looked pretty great from right field.

It is on these miniature baseball fields that some of us experienced the greatest exhilaration in our young lives (as well as some of our greatest embarrassments). Seeing my buddy Wayne hit a grounder back to the pitcher and make a beeline for third base instead of first base, as everybody looked on in amazement and then fell into convulsive laughter, was an all-time winner for me, and it is still the standard by which I measure embarrassing moments.

It is here that we discover that good guys don't always finish last—or first, either. Being a good guy simply has nothing to do with it. We learn that "winning is not the most important thing, it's the only thing," and other foolish sayings. The discerning parent looks on somewhat sadly and is reminded that God seems to distribute talent, oftentimes, to the most undeserving—meaning anybody's kid but yours. As we play the game and watch the pros, a lot of it just doesn't make any sense. Often a skinny little guy can throw the ball harder than the bigger, more muscular guy. Baseball reminds me of those mysterious ancient monuments that we see on the Discovery Channel that are perfectly aligned with heavenly bodies so as to produce sundials and perfect patterns that can only be seen from great heights, fostering speculation that the world was visited many years ago by aliens from another planet. In baseball, the bases are spaced so that countless plays involving runners of different speeds are decided by a fraction of a second.

A batter can hit the ball hard—in fact, perfectly—but right at a fielder, making an out. Another batter can hit a weak pop-up, but perfectly placed by accident, and gets a hit, raising his all-important batting average. We assume that the gods of baseball have it all worked out and that there's a rough justice to it all that we aren't meant to understand. So, on second thought, in many respects the metaphor-mongers are right: Baseball is a lot like life.

The photographs in the weekly *Democrat Union*, Lawrenceburg's only newspaper, displayed the first organized Little League baseball teams to ever take the field in Lawrenceburg. There I was, a proud, somewhat chubby, twelve-year-old member of the Lions in my own ill-fitting uniform. The "Roaring Lions" we were christened by "The Bald-headed Brothers," the photography shop in town. (Talk about marketing savvy. I still remember what they called themselves over fifty years later. Somewhat wasted, I suppose, since as I said, they were the only photographers in town.) The Roaring Lions roared to victory twice that season. Weak at the plate, we offset it by total incompetence in the field. Not exactly deep in talent to begin with, we lost our best player by far early in the year. After our tryouts for team selection, it seemed that our manager had used most of his allotted points on "draft day" on a real potential all-star named Everette, leaving him with fewer points to select the rest of the team. But Everette, perhaps the best hitter in the league and one of the best pitchers, could do it all. However, the coach, having put all his eggs in one basket, ran afoul of a common country code. You don't fuss on another man's kid—especially in public, which is what our manager did one night when Everette made a baserunning error and was called out. I suppose the manager was especially disappointed because he realized that Everette was probably the only kid on the team who had a real chance of getting on base. The criticism wasn't really a big deal except to Everette's family. Everette's dad came out onto the field, got his boy, and left, leaving us to stew in our own mediocrity. The result: two wins, and many, many more losses.

The manager assigned me to third base—for no apparent reason, I suppose, other than I probably looked like I could throw the ball across the diamond to first base. The coach was partially correct. I could throw the ball in the *general direction* of first base. Just about any position would have been fine with me; I'd gotten over my disappointment of missing out on my first choice of position. At the tryouts, when the guy in charge hollered at all of us to identify ourselves by position, he started out by saying, "All right, how many pitchers do we have here?" Of the sixty to seventy boys present, probably fifty of us raised our hand. My choice didn't survive the first tryout.

The sad fact is that after Everette left, very few of us could—as Dad delicately put it one time when describing a ballplayer—hit a bull in the butt with a bass fiddle (sometimes I envisioned that description right after I struck out).

However, I had already established myself as a "glove man." It was opening night. I got dressed in my uniform about four hours before the game. When we got there, it was midway through the first game and there was what looked like a big crowd and it was under the lights. It was wonderful. I remember it all very clearly. In the first inning, a batter popped up to me at third base. Gosh, he hit it high. The noise of the crowd, the pressure—I moved around, trying to get under it. It must have been in the air for five minutes as I stumbled around. Then, miraculously, the ball made contact with my glove. I had actually caught it! The exhilaration was indescribable. It was my first big test in organized athletics, and I had passed. That catch saw me through numerous errors and losses that year. No matter. Whatever else happened, I'd always have "the catch."

My passion for baseball had been solidified at the age of twelve. It was 1954, the year that the Cleveland Indians won the American League pennant. They were my favorite team throughout my boyhood. How did a kid from rural Tennessee become a rabid fan of the Cleveland Indians? Most baseball loyalties are born in traditional ways—a kid's hometown or regional team, your dad's team, or the team of your favorite player that you saw on TV. But we had no teams in the South and no baseball on television. This gaping hole was filled for me by the fact that my aunt Juanita, my mother's sister, lived in Cleveland with her husband. That summer, Ma and Pa Bradley, Mom, and I drove to visit Juanita and her family. But it wasn't as uncomplicated as it sounds.

First of all, the trip was in part a reconnaissance mission. Juanita had been acting strangely. At least, that's the way she seemed on the phone and in her letters. She had married a Yankee from Cleveland. Worse than that, a Yankee from Czechoslovakia and we couldn't pronounce his last name. He was a perfectly nice fellow, but he had two strikes against him, and Juanita was acting like she was perfectly happy to live in Cleveland, Ohio, with this Czechoslovakian Yankee. Clearly, something was amiss, so we headed north.

After the long, un-air-conditioned drive, we approached Cleveland much as American troops probably approached the Anbar Province. When we arrived, without incurring enemy fire, we learned that the living quarters situation was less than ideal for company. In fact, looking back on it, I'm not sure my folks told Juanita that we were even coming. Juanita and her husband, Frank, had just opened a little diner with three rooms. The part of the diner that was open had just one little row of stools with a countertop across a grill. Frank had two grown sons, who were fixing up an adjoining room for the diner, and the family was living in another room. We stayed at a motel.

Of course, with Frank trying to start his own business, it was the worst possible time for his in-laws to descend on him. Hot dogs and ice cream were about all that was served, and I thought I'd died and gone to heaven as I sat there on the stool every day deciding whether I wanted another hot dog, and helping eat away at what little profits they were earning at the time.

In addition to his tolerance, Frank did something else that left a lasting impression on me. He took our family to two Cleveland Indians night games. This was before the day when a man had to take out a second mortgage if he wanted to treat his family to a major-league baseball game. I think each of our tickets was about $1.25, but it still must have been a bit of a sacrifice. I wonder if a guy like Frank could spring for the ticket prices today, plus food and drinks. Even accounting for inflation, I suspect that a lot of little boys like me are not making it to the park these days. However, *other* boys were the last thing on my mind that first night.

The Indians were playing the Boston Red Sox at Cleveland's old Municipal Stadium. We entered the ballpark and walked through the crowded, somewhat dark passageway around to the entrance leading to our seats. Then we walked out into the brightly lit, vast expanse of openness. There was a beautifully manicured green field below us and people in unending rows of seats, billboards and music surrounding us. It took my breath away. I absorbed every sight, sound, and smell that was there that night. I sometimes have trouble remembering my telephone number, but I still remember the starting lineup of the 1954 Indians.

As I often tried to explain in my youth, it wasn't as if I wasn't learning. I was just learning different stuff. Anyway, Lawrenceburg, Tennessee, had at least one Cleveland Indians fan, and I suffered the true sports fan's exhilaration and heartache when they won the American League pennant that year but lost the World Series in four straight to the New York Giants. Pinch hitter Dusty Rhodes (in those days, everyone named Rhodes was called "Dusty") killed us with two home runs.

I watched the World Series that year for the first time on

television at my grandma Thompson's house, since she and Pa Thompson sprung for a TV before Dad and Mom did. Ma Thompson's primary interest in buying a TV was because of *Wrestling from Hollywood.* I am not kidding. When one of the heroes like Freddie Blassie would throttle one of the villains like Gorgeous George, then put a triple dropkick on him, she would jump up and exclaim along with the announcer, "Whoa, Nellie!" She especially loved the midget Indian wrestlers when they would come out in their headgear doing war whoops. At Ma Thompson's, I never worried about being exposed to *Masterpiece Theater* or its equivalent, and that suited me fine. For Ma Thompson and me, it was either midget wrestlers or something involving a ball.

This was during the time when an important social issue was beginning to be reflected on the sports field. By 1954, Larry Doby, the first black player in the American League, was playing center field for the Cleveland Indians. Therefore, he became one of my favorites. However, that was not enough to raise my social consciousness with regard to my own world. Playing Little League, for example, it never did occur to us that we didn't have any black players on our team, or any of the opposing teams, for that matter.

This would have been in the period when "separate but equal" was accepted, and that meant the majority of black kids in our community were bused about twenty-three miles to the Mt. Pleasant community to go to school. For us kids, that was just a fact of life; we didn't think much about it.

That didn't stop us from competing. Some black teenagers had a pretty good baseball team, and some of us formed a team to play them. In all the games we played against each other, there were never any issues except some good-natured ribbing. One day we were playing and we had a middle-aged black fellow serving as umpire behind home plate, calling balls and strikes. I was up to bat. By then I was a lanky six feet, three inches or so. The pitcher threw a pitch that was probably three or four inches off the ground, and the umpire called it a strike. "That ball was barely off the ground. My knees are way up here," I yelped, pointing to my knees as if he couldn't see them.

Quick as a wink, he replied, "I can't help it, buddy, I didn't make you." I don't recall if I got a hit, but I laughed off and on for a couple of innings. I couldn't wait to tell Dad, who naturally thought it was as funny as I did.

I could sense things changing, though in other ways. In high school during one summer, I worked for the "city" cutting grass along the highway with a "sling blade." (I wondered why every little incorporated community in Tennessee called itself a "city" no matter how small the population. I guess "city police department" sounded better than "wide spot in the road police department." But I digress.) One of my fellow members on the city "chain gang" was a black boy named Bobby, who was about my age. He was a nice enough guy, but he acted like something was on his mind all the time. He seemed studious and serious about his work, and I had assumed that he would be happy-go-lucky like I was. His demeanor registered with me, and I'd started to piece it all together.

The evolution in a lot of people's thinking got a big assist from an unlikely source. Segregation was about to collide with another Southern institution: football. In this battle, segregation didn't stand a chance. Bear Bryant, the legendary coach of Alabama, saw it coming and welcomed it. Alabama had won national championships in 1961, 1964, and 1965 with all-white teams, and of course that's the way people wanted it—in fact, they insisted upon it. However, the Alabama teams began to falter after that. In 1970, Bryant put Southern California, an integrated team, on the schedule to play in Birmingham. A black Southern Cal running back, Clarence Davis, who was originally from Birmingham, along with another black running back named Sam Cunningham, ran roughshod over Alabama and beat them 42–21. Cunningham scored three touchdowns. Pretty soon, Bryant was allowed to recruit black players for Alabama (and started winning again). Bryant said, "Sam Cunningham did more to integrate Alabama in one afternoon than Martin Luther King had in years."

"The Bear" might be forgiven for his overstatement, but

in one way or another over the next several years, whether due to self-interest, habit, or law, people began to think differently about what was right and fair.

Though good people can sometimes have a large blind spot in their value system, it was hard for the folks I knew to be mean and unkind when they literally had to come face-to-face with the result of some long-held beliefs and assumptions. We didn't realize that a social transition was going on, even though we were living right in the middle of it. I guess that is especially true if you are busy just growing up and think you have your own serious problems to worry about. My generation saw the complete changing of certain basic notions. I went from a time when almost everyone I knew thought that separation of the races was the natural order of things to a time when almost everyone I knew thought exactly the opposite. That's quite a journey. And it's one that thankfully my home folks and I, along with a lot of other Americans, made together.

During grade school there was no organized football in Lawrenceburg, so we would just take our game of disorganized mayhem to the backyards and playgrounds on our side of town—tackle football with no pads. It was mainly a lot of grabbing, shoving, and running headlong into one another, sort of like a session of the Italian Parliament.

Lawrenceburg Public did have a basketball team. As much

as I would have loved to, I knew better than to try out for the team. They didn't need a slow-footed kid of average height and marginal shooting ability. However, I did have one basketball-related thrill in grade school. It lasted all of about thirty seconds. My class was in the basement classroom of Miss Sadie, our music teacher. Miss Sadie's job was to teach music without the benefit of musical instruments, except for her piano, to mostly farm kids and other uninterested captives. My own musical exposure extended to listening to the Grand Ole Opry on the radio on Saturday nights with Dad. When I was younger, my folks had taken me to the Opry to see Hank Williams, Sr., sing Dad's favorite, "Lovesick Blues," and I still remember the lyrics. Unfortunately, never once in the ensuing years was "Lovesick Blues" or the Cleveland Indians' lineup ever the answer to any exam question.

In class we did a lot of "singing" to Miss Sadie's accompaniment, learning about what a "sharp" and "flat" look like in a songbook, along with something about "beats to a measure." What that has to do with music we hadn't a clue (and I still don't).

For some reason, most days Miss Sadie didn't seem to be very happy. Let's just say that Miss Sadie's personality reflected her lot in life. In addition to apparently not liking kids, Miss Sadie had this weird hangup about Santa Claus. She insisted that his name should be pronounced as if it were "Santy" Claus. So when we sang "Santa Claus Is Coming to

Town," she would stop the music and it would be "No, no, I told you it's 'Santy' Claus. Sant*y*, Sant*y*. Okay, once again."

Of course, most of us aspiring musicians sang even louder, "Santa Claus is coming to town."

"No, no, no," she'd say, and we'd start all over again.

We had heard that, as a younger woman, she was very pleasant and perfectly sane. We couldn't figure out what had happened to her.

Anyway, basketball practice was at the same time as Miss Sadie's class, and kids on the team were excused from class. We boys knew that Coach Webb had been watching us play basketball at recess. My buddy, Bob, was a good shooter and probably should have been on the basketball team from the beginning. One day after he had sunk a couple of long ones at recess, a kid knocked on Miss Sadie's classroom door, came in, and announced that Mr. Webb wanted Bob to report to him at the gym. We knew that Bob had been summoned for the basketball team.

I saw Bob's ascendancy with decidedly mixed emotions. Well, actually, I was bitterly disappointed. Bob, and not I, had been rescued from musical purgatory for the glory and adulation that came with being an LPS Basketball Cherokee. Deep down, I knew it was never meant to be. However, a few minutes later my envy turned to total exhilaration. Bob knocked on the door and said that he needed me to come with him. I jumped up. I and everyone else knew that Mr. Webb was calling for me, too. At least, we thought we knew. As soon as we got out the door, Bob said, "Freddie, I need to borrow your gym shoes. I didn't bring any today." I told him where I put them in the cloakroom and slunk back into Miss Sadie's classroom just as they were singing another verse of "Go Tell Aunt Rhody (That the Old Gray Goose Is Dead)." The song seemed appropriate. I sat there in disgrace, knowing that my athletic career was over before it began.

Nevertheless, I was determined to "keep in shape." For what purpose I did not know. But after church on summer nights, at my request Dad would let me out of the car and I would run home trailing the car, as Dad kept a slow pace. I suppose the neighbors wondered, "What has that Thompson boy done now to deserve this?" Actually, I was doing more than keeping in shape—I wanted to change my body from the sort of pear shape that it was in.

The rites of passage are not easy for a kid who is on the outer edges of the talent pool. More to the point, you have to take a certain amount of abuse. For example, in our pickup football games, when you reached a certain level you got to "center for both sides" because nobody wanted to play center. They wanted to pass, run, or catch the ball. You don't do any of that when you play center. In fact, when you centered the ball, while you still had your head between your legs, the boy on the other side would pull you forward into the ground while everyone would run over you. Soon you got smart enough to invoke the "no-ducking rule" before the game started. The rule was consistently breached, but it allowed you to retain the moral high ground in the argument that invariably ensued. It made you feel better about your bloody nose or whatever.

The older boys invented other imaginative miseries that would be seasonably appropriate. During basketball season they came up with a game euphemistically called "Bump." We would take turns shooting from a specific spot. If you missed a shot, you had to bend over under the goal with your hands on your knees while the others, from a running start, took turns throwing the basketball at your backside as hard as they could. Considering my shooting ability and the size of the target that I presented, it made for some long afternoons for me.

But to me I was becoming a "player" both figuratively and literally. One might ask, Why in the world would a kid subject himself to such treatment? It reminds me of the story of the fellow at the circus who would walk around behind the elephants with a pooper-scooper and clean up after them. When asked why in the world he did not quit such a terrible job, his reply was "What, and leave show business?"

In Nashville my eighth-grade class had a softball team, but I didn't go out for it. I tried to pretend I wasn't interested, but the team seemed pretty well set when I got there and I didn't see much chance of breaking into the lineup. This way they couldn't say I didn't make the team.

But that year something remarkable started to happen. I began to grow. And grow. I went from slightly above-average height to well over six feet tall. I'd also lost any signs of my little-boy chubbiness. I began my freshman year and could have sworn that a girl smiled at me for no apparent reason. I started to look into the mirror on a regular basis and finally had to face it. I was a hoss. A stud. It was happening. Never mind that that year's annual picture showed a gangly, slightly goofy-looking kid with a bad haircut. As everyone knows, photographs can be deceiving. I was getting feedback, man. I started doubling down on a rusty old barbell that Dad had come up with from somewhere.

Still, progress was slow. My freshman year, I got nowhere in basketball and worked my way up to second-string center in football. Yes, still playing center. My superiors, the coaches this time, were apparently still looking for someone who was willing to play a good part of the game with his head between his legs. Ducking the center had just been replaced by a steady diet of forearm blows to the top of my helmet, and occasionally my face, by the fellow opposite me. Of course, this is practice I am talking about. I was never put into a game.

Midway through my sophomore year, it all began to change. I had grown to six feet, five inches and was developing a little coordination. I was working hard. I had the advantage of not being distracted by less important considerations, such as schoolwork. That was going to take care of itself, I thought. I'd heard a talk one day in class about "osmosis," which really stuck with me. I was counting on it getting me through school. But back to the important stuff.

I was one of only two sophomores to make the varsity basketball team. Actually, sightings of me on a basketball court during a game were rare that year, but riding that school bus to all those little country towns to away games was exciting enough for me for the time being. Sitting on the bench gave me a chance to get used to the crowd pressure in some of those gymnasiums. And I'm not just talking about the decibel level. In some of those old country gyms, the sideline was about one foot from the beginning of the bleachers. In order to inbound a ball, you'd have to fix your feet in among the spectators and not be distracted by an occasional pinch or the pulling of the hair on your leg as you were trying to get the ball in bounds. Of course, our home crowd presented its own challenges. I learned one night that you don't actually have to be in the game in order to get embarrassed. We were leading by a comfortable margin when a bunch of the students started chanting, "We want Freddie, we want Freddie." I sat on the bench, grinning, trying to adopt an aw-shucks attitude.

As they persisted, Coach Staggs finally called me over from the other end of the bench. I threw off my warm-up jacket and ran to him. He looked at me straight in the face and said, "Do you hear what they're yelling—that they want you?" "Yes, sir," I replied. With that he pointed to the crowd and said, "All right, go on over there with them," and laughed. As the crowd howled, I sheepishly walked back down to the end of the bench and tried to act like I was in on the joke. All I could do was smile and think, "Okay, that's one for you guys." However, it did teach me something about cool. If you want something really badly, try not to show it. Otherwise, you're going to get messed with.

The next year it all came together. I had filled out to about 185 pounds of dangerous muscle. However, I had to be doubly impressive in order to overcome an obstacle to my success—my mouth—and a penchant to find humor where others less clever failed to see it.

My first day of summer practice I couldn't find my gym socks and showed up for practice in my high-top shoes with no socks, looking even more like a backwoods Ichabod Crane. Then our coach gave us a somewhat emotional speech, which I thought was funny since it was only a prelude to running us until our tongues hung out. During warm-ups I yelled for the boys to bear down. "Let's get serious, guys," I said. "After all, we've got a game in six months." A verbal lashing ensued, and after that for some reason the coaching staff thought my attitude wasn't exactly what it should be. Of course, my attitude toward football was just fine. I just didn't see what that had to do with passing up a good line.

They say that if a kid doesn't think his high school coach hung the moon, then there is something wrong with either the boy or the coach. I felt that way about Coach Staggs. He was looked upon with fear and awe because of his exalted position in our eyes and because of his demeanor, which was sort of like Captain Ahab without the humor. He was simply the gatekeeper to the most important thing in our lives at the time, and he commanded respect. No one doubted the story about the player who was out behind the ag building one day when Coach was seen approaching. He ate the cigarette he had been smoking.

The funny thing about it was that Coach was about five feet, six inches tall. Behind his back (and I mean *way* behind his back) some of the seniors called him Stumpy. A creative player from years gone by had come up with this one: "Do you know why Stumpy sued the city? Answer: Because they built the sidewalk too close to his butt." From a rough childhood he had become a high school phenom as a running back from the mean streets of Nashville. He went on to Ole Miss on a football scholarship. He was Red Grange, as far as I was concerned. He didn't like smart alecks, comics, or individualists. You can see what I was up against. He had strict rules on and off the field. For example, there would be no water on the football field during a game or during practice, and we had plenty of ninety-plus-degree days under a Tennessee sun.

These and other things that today would have the coach up before the United Nations on charges of human rights violations were not uncommon back in the day. It's amazing how kids nowadays seem to be able to play almost as well as we did while still getting a drink of water.

I found that the coaches would overlook a certain number of indiscretions if you knocked enough people on their butt. Another wonderful lesson I was learning. While I was not very fast, I discovered that by employing a rather sophisticated technique I could make up for it. They tried me at defensive end and discovered that from a standing upright start I could crash the opposing backfield to great effect. I would run headlong into a group of blockers and disrupt whatever they were trying to do. I didn't even have to make the tackle. My teammates could mop that up. Pretty sophisticated, huh? I've seen athletes on TV thank the Lord for their "God-given talent." Well, this was my God-given talent. Occasionally, I could even grab the runner on the way by.

As a junior, my newly discovered skill earned me a starting position on the defensive line. I felt that I had died and gone to heaven. And I wasn't going to let little things distract me—little things like permanent disfigurement.

This particular distraction came in the form of my old nemesis, Joe Plunkett. Every boy seems to have one growing up, and Joe was mine. Hopefully, most boys are smart enough not to have a nemesis who started shaving at age twelve. Joe was a senior, and he was still tough. We'd had at least three major encounters over the years. By encounters I mean fights where blood was shed—usually mine.

Anyway, beyond having my starting defensive-line job, I had the added responsibility of centering for punts and extra points for the team. Joe was the punter. One day on the practice field we got into an argument about something. Naturally, as any fool would do, I pulled off my helmet equipped with face mask. As I went for his legs, Joe adroitly grabbed the back of my shoulder pads and pulled me forward and down onto the ground, causing my face to plow up enough turf to plant a nice row of beans.

However, all I actually planted was two of my front teeth—one tooth and about a third of another, to be precise. The thing I most vividly remember about this episode is how utterly narrow-minded a boy's mother can be about such situations. It seems to take a mother to point out that, even though you may be acting like a six-year-old, teeth don't grow back when you are a teenager. Mom was heartbroken. She probably also felt that I didn't need any additional disadvantages as far as my personal appearance was concerned.

My coaches were concerned, too. Sensitive guys as they were, they asked me if I was still going to be willing to stick my head in there. Of course I'd stick my head in there. After all, nothing of particular value was at stake—just my head. Besides, this was a chance to prove my toughness. Also, there was an upside that nobody had counted on. Due to the state of dental technology at the time—at least in Lawrenceburg—I not only got a false replacement tooth but the third of the other tooth was capped with gold! Hot dang! Gold on my front tooth, just like Dad's from his encounter with a deputy sheriff when Dad wasn't much older than I was. As proud as I was, it did occur to me that we Thompsons ought to learn a lesson from this legacy—we ought to learn how to fight a little better. But as far as I was concerned, the gold tooth was only adding to the legend.

Football season started and I did fine. In fact, I was named Schoolboy Star of the Week in Middle Tennessee after one game. But it was like when things were going well I always seemed to want to spice them up a little bit. I guess a young man's heritage is bound to catch up with him every once in a while. One Friday night in Fayetteville, Tennessee, during a play a guy's finger stuck me in the eye. I had never felt anything so painful. After the play, I was doubled over on the ground trying to decide if I was going to be blind. Although the pain was short-lived, the referees stopped the game and our managers ran out to check on my condition. Everyone was huddled around me, wondering how badly I was hurt. I couldn't help it. I looked up, grinning, and said, "How are the fans taking it?" I think it's fair to say the coaches were not amused. It would also be correct to say that to this day I am known more in Lawrenceburg by some of my old friends for this incident than anything else I ever did on a football field.

We lost only one or two games that year and were rewarded for our efforts by being selected for a bowl game. We were the top team in Middle Tennessee, and we got to go to the Butter Bowl in Pulaski. Some of our farm boys on the team could have probably walked there with no problem. Pulaski was eighteen miles down the road. We won the game handily. Capping off a very good year, I was selected Honorable Mention All Mid State. I could hardly wait for the next football season to begin the following year, when I would be one of the few starters to return. I knew that, with the increased weight I would pick up, glory days were right around the corner.

But first there was basketball season, which actually started before we finished playing football. The beginning of the season was not a pretty picture, because most of the basketball players were also football players. Putting a bunch of rawboned country boys on the basketball court with no practice is problematic at best. Add to that the fact that they'd been playing football for several months, and it's all knees, elbows, and sliding on the floor. But before long, it was obvious that we were going to have a very good team.

The team was made up of mostly seniors, including Joe Plunkett, who played under the basket, where it became very dangerous for the opposition to tread—a fact to which I could personally attest. (Joe and I later became good friends before he tragically died while still in his twenties.) I was the sixth man on the team, and I played a lot once I got over my football tendencies, which was not easy. One night early in the season, Coach Staggs put me into the game, and I got fourteen points in a little over a quarter. The bad news was I also fouled out. Coach decided he needed me in smaller doses—perhaps in more ways than one.

We qualified for the state tournament. This, my friends, was a really big deal—especially for those on our team who had never seen a tall building before. This may be stretching it a little, but the word was that during the tournament you could tell country boys from the country schools. They were the ones over at Harvey's Department Store putting their chewing gum on the escalator so they could watch it come back around again.

This was the big stage—at Vanderbilt University. The gymnasium was cavernous and unique even among college gyms, with the court extending several feet beyond the out-of-bounds line before you reached the first row of seats, which were below court level. It's like the court was a huge stage. I remember double-checking to make sure I had put on my basketball shorts under my warm-up pants. I could hear the huge crowd from our dressing room. Other guys were checking, too. I guess it was kind of like a paratrooper checking his chute one last time before his first jump.

Of course, as I have discovered in other forums since then, it's surprising how quick the crowd and noise all blend into the background once the work starts. Things turned out pretty well for us. We won the first game and lost in the second round, leaving us fourth in the state. In those days, there were no school classifications according to size. The smallest schools competed with the biggest, so fourth in the state was a significant achievement. Bowl game in football and fourth in the state in basketball. Not bad for country boys, and it really set the stage for next year and a scholarship offer— probably for football. I had heard that my coaches thought that would happen. Of course, I had little interest in the scholarship part. I just wanted to play, and a man's got to make certain sacrifices.

Swapping Old Dreams
for New Ones

ANOTHER HAPPY BY-PRODUCT of my growing confidence was that my own social standing seemed to be improving.

Sarah Lindsey and her girlfriends, for example, were at the top of the high school pecking order in terms of looks, grades, and musical talent. She was a senior and I was a junior. When we met at a Halloween party at school, it was clear to me that she was as sweet as she was pretty, and for some reason she liked me. Our first date was after a night football game, as a teammate buddy of mine, Tommy Morrow, had his dad's car and we decided to double-date. We were looking for some way to impress the girls, and fortunately a solution was readily at hand. Bobby Alford was a high school sports fan and a baseball coach of mine who was not much older than we were. In those days, Bobby was a little on the heavy side, and we, being the sensitive and imaginative guys that we were, nicknamed him "Fat."

Fat Alford had various side ventures, including a little hog-raising operation in a vacant lot just outside of town, and we would go with him to check on the hogs from time to time. Naturally, Tommy and I thought that a visit to Fat's hog pen would be a great way to impress these city girls. We tromped around all over the place, pointing out the better features as well as the habits of the fine specimens shining before us in the moonlight. Actually, I think that was the last date that Tommy ever had with his girl, but fortunately Sarah was a little more broad-minded. From Fat's hog pen, this unlikely couple (Sarah and me) were off to an improbable start that would change both of our lives.

That summer I was hired as a lifeguard at the city swimming pool after passing a rigorous examination.

"Do you swim?"

"Yeah."

"You're hired."

I lifted weights, dated Sarah, and prepared for my "break-out" senior year in football. Sarah had received an academic scholarship to Peabody in Nashville, where she planned to embark on a teaching career. She had already graduated, but we had it all worked out, with plans to see each other on weekends while I finished high school.

Before school started, football practice was in full gear during the hot and humid Tennessee summer nights. During our first scrimmage, I went downfield and threw a block on a defensive back. I went too low and drove my shoulder into the ground. That was effectively the end of football for me. The shoulder was "separated," they said, but all I knew was that it just never seemed to get better. I spent the rest of the summer in preseason practice with my arm in a sling. Every time I tested it out on the field, I would hurt it again. I was distraught. The one thing that I was good at had been taken away from me. My future accomplishments were tied to a football scholarship that was now very much in doubt; I thought that my life was being changed forever. I didn't know the half of it.

Sarah and I had long since fallen very much in love. I suppose one has to smile when hearing that about seventeen- and eighteen-year-olds. "They can't know anything about love." Turns out we did. Although we were both inexperienced in such things, we just simply couldn't imagine not being together. It seemed that simple. But, of course, it was not that simple.

I don't remember when Sarah first told me, but I do remember our drive down to Florence, Alabama, forty miles south of Lawrenceburg, to get a doctor's verification. I especially remember her coming out of the doctor's office with tears rolling down her cheeks as I waited in the reception area.

At the supper table that night, Dad asked me what I had done that day. That's all it took. I broke down and told Mom and Dad everything. Of course, they were very upset, but their reaction was immediately one of love and support.

They were calm. From that moment it was all about the future. We all realized that my boyhood was now at an end. For Dad and me, it was man-to-man. We would work it out. One thing was assumed by all of us. Sarah and I would get married. It was never really discussed. It wasn't a matter of if, but when.

After all the cards were on the table, I don't remember ever once feeling afraid or distraught. Sarah would not be able to go to Peabody, but that just meant that we would be together. That's what we had planned all along. We were just moving up the timetable. The only anguish I felt was years later when my children became our ages back then. It was then that I realized how very, very young we were and what our parents had gone through.

Our youth and lack of knowledge protected us in a way. Because we could not foresee all the difficulties that lay ahead, when they did rise up we just assumed they were a normal part of life. Without the foreboding, there is a lot less unhappiness, regardless of what happens. It is something I have tried to remember. Somehow, we were ready for whatever was in store for us. We were married in September 1959. I had turned seventeen the month before. We were married for twenty-five years before divorcing.

We went to Florence, Alabama, for an overnight honeymoon, and our car broke down the next day on our way back to Lawrenceburg. We hitchhiked back to town. It's amazing the things that don't embarrass you to death when you are seventeen years old. Yes, sir, I was quite a catch.

Part of the plan was for me to finish high school. I didn't expect confetti and a marching band when I returned to school, but I also wasn't expecting what I did experience upon my return. Even though my maturity had progressed somewhat, I had no reservoir of goodwill to fall back on with the coach when first I got injured and then when the world found out I was going to be a daddy.

After I hurt my shoulder and couldn't play, I was not allowed to ride on the team bus to the away games—no use filling a seat with a spectator. I could still play basketball, but after I got married, instead of letting the team elect a captain, as was the custom, Coach appointed the only other senior on the team to fill that role. All the guys knew what was going on, and the rejection and embarrassment of the coach's actions toward me were painful.

I had expected the coach to look past the record before him and see that I was basically a well-meaning kid who was being forced to grow up a lot faster than I might have wanted. But he clearly saw no redeeming value in me. And to be fair, I hadn't given him much cause to see beyond his limited perceptions.

A person is judged on the basis of what they do, not on what they think about themselves, and potential can earn you only so much credit, until that potential runs out or is wasted. If you don't go about things the proper way, you'd better be prepared when times get tough, because there probably won't be much of a wellspring of sympathy for you to draw upon. I had not earned the coach's trust or his good-will. So when I was no longer productive as an athlete, he had no need for me. And, although he could have handled it better, I had no right to expect him to see what I thought was my potential. He was a good man using what skills he had at his disposal. But there is no greater motivator than the burning desire to show somebody that they were wrong about you. In a very short time, my circumstances had led me to create a pretty long list of folks to prove wrong; I added Coach to that list.

Naturally, I have sometimes wondered what would have happened if I hadn't torn up my shoulder. Would I have gotten that scholarship? If so, which school would I have attended? Would I have made the team and had great success? I'll never know the answers, but I do know one thing. These things that may have seemed like tragedies at the time were the best things that could have happened to me.

After Winston Churchill had led Great Britain and the free world to victory in World War II, the English people turned their back on him and he was defeated in his bid for reelection as prime minister. His wife supposedly said to him, "Winston, perhaps it is a blessing in disguise." To which he replied, "Yes, very heavily disguised." So it was for me. But I was doubly blessed. I really never had to face up to the fact that I probably was not good enough to be outstanding. I could always be an all-star in my imagination, but more importantly, getting married saved me from wasting at least a few years of my life. I know now that I simply wouldn't have made it academically and I wouldn't have developed a sense of responsibility until I absolutely had to. When my basketball coach informed me that having a married man on the team wasn't a very good idea and it would be best if I left the team, I did not argue with him. I was ready to move on.

Welcome to
the Real World

A<small>S MIGHT BE EXPECTED,</small> not all of Lawrenceburg's denizens shared my optimism for our future. One of Sarah's mother's friends was heard to say, "I am afraid Sarah Elizabeth has led her ducks to a dry pond." It became quite obvious that this assessment was shared by most of Sarah's family. Her mother was a Southern lady, gracious and kind, and coped the best of them all. Her father, Oscar, was the quiet and steady cornerstone of a family of extroverts and achievers. He was building a grand new colonial home on the outskirts of town, with a bedroom and dressing room suite for Sarah—rooms that even years later never saw a piece of furniture. I can imagine what he thought every time he looked at me, which was not often.

Oscar and his older brother, Ed, had started making furniture in their garage as boys, and from that they built a small but thriving church-furniture operation. One night after Sarah and I had made our announcement to our parents,

Oscar and I had our first discussion about my plans for the future. As one might expect, it was a short discussion. I told him I had a Sunday-morning paper route delivering the *Nashville Tennessean* to rural mailboxes by car, and that I had thought about being an athletics coach. We agreed that I would work at the factory after school, stacking lumber and sanding furniture. And Sarah and I would live with the Lindseys while I finished my senior year in high school.

During this time and for years after, Oscar and I spent many postdinner hours watching television or reading in the same room, seldom ever exchanging a word. I am talking hours of silence. I never knew how much of it was due to his nature and how much was because of the circumstances. In larger family gatherings, when he would speak, I was able to get a read on his thinking, and what he said sometimes had more than a little impact on me. He had an insight and a way of looking at things that sometimes differed from the thinking that I was used to.

Along with being a businessman, Oscar was also a captain in the Tennessee National Guard and in charge of several men who trained at the local armory. One night over dinner, he mentioned that an incident between some of the men had taken place at the armory and that it had had some racial overtones. He paused, as if weighing his words, then he said, "You know, if I were a black man, I would be the meanest one there ever was."

Maybe it was because he was one of few members of his

family who was not a politician. Or maybe he was not a politician because of some of the things he believed. All in all, over the years it became obvious to me that he was one of the best men I had ever known, and despite my occasional resentment, it was important to me to gain his respect. I had a lot of work to do—with him as well as the rest of the family.

Sarah's uncle Ed was a dynamo. With only a high school education, he had become the mayor of Lawrenceburg, the Mayor of the Year in Tennessee, and the International President of the Lions Club. He and his wife, Virginia, traveled the world, and he was often mentioned for statewide office, although he never made the run. Never have I seen two brothers who were more different and more compatible than Oscar and Ed. Ed was gregarious, outgoing, and a great public speaker. During Ed's travels Oscar ran the business, which had grown to thirty or forty employees. He was happy for Ed to have the limelight. Sarah's uncle, A.D., was a lawyer and had been the county judge, which is the chief executive officer of the county. Her uncle Bid was an Alcohol, Tobacco, and Firearms agent and had been a star athlete. He was the most friendly of "the boys."

The head of the Lindsey clan was Sarah's grandfather, "Pap," who was also a lawyer. He was tall and straight, with a full head of white hair. Town folks called him "The Judge," although he had never actually been one. He just seemed like he should have been one. He was from the old school that believed in shooting first and asking questions later—literally. There was a story that once he got up in the middle of the night, saw a stranger out in the backyard, and filled full of buckshot a perfectly innocent pair of long johns hanging on the clothesline. He walked to and from his office every day until he was well into his eighties. Often after supper the boys and their families would convene at Pap's house and pass judgment on the politicians and settle the world's problems. Pap was one of the relatively few Republicans in town. Ed, A.D., and Oscar had joined the Democrats in order to not foreclose political opportunities in the heavily Democratic county.

I learned when the subject of Sarah and me had first come up at a family meeting that my name had met with less-than-enthusiastic support. In fact, the board of uncles subscribed to the "ducks to the pond" analysis totally. However, after everyone had had their say, Pap rendered his verdict: "If Sarah sees something in this boy, then there must be something there." That was the end of that. I was going to be in the family and I would have a seat at the table. Before long I was listening to the discussions and even chiming in from time to time. And I was learning about politics, current events, and old courtroom war stories. Mainly, I was learning about myself. This was interesting stuff. I thought maybe I was not as dumb as the evidence would indicate.

To my delight, I soon realized that Pap was taking me under his wing.

Pap lived next door to us, and often I would go over and we would continue our conversations as he smoked his pipe. Just the two of us. Other times, I'd go over and sit on the porch with one of his old, outdated law books. I could not for a second comprehend the concepts in those books, but I wanted to know the things that he knew about.

Given the men she had grown up with, there was not a day that went by that I didn't feel the need to prove myself to Sarah; I knew that, whether she knew it or not, she would always be measuring me against them. This was now my focus.

The next April, Sarah gave birth to a beautiful little boy. Sarah wanted to name him after me. I wanted to call him Tony. So we did both. My name is not Frederick but "Freddie." While a fine name for a little boy, Mom said later that it did not occur to her or Dad that it might not be too appealing to a grown man. However, I acceded to Sarah's wishes that we name him Freddie Dalton Thompson II instead of Jr. I didn't like "Junior," and I didn't know that the "II" was not normally used for one's own children. Thus, I succeeded in adding my own unique naming scheme to the "Freddie" offense that had been visited upon me. Happily, Tony, now a lawyer in the Nashville area, has been able to overcome it successfully and keeps any grudges to himself.

All of this does add to the argument that everyone should be allowed to grow up and name themselves.

I was getting an expedited course on growing up. But it was not as if I was a passenger on a train who had looked up and suddenly found himself in a foreign land. I was more like a passenger who had barely noticed the foggy scenery quickly move by but then looked up and saw that he was out of the fog and into the clear. I found myself in a good place where I felt I was meant to be. I had the girl I loved and the miracle of this little boy whom I adored. I also had the eyes of everyone on me. I had to try to make something out of myself. I just didn't know what it was going to be.

Sarah and I had already decided that our next step was going to be college. The nearest and probably least expensive one was Florence State College in Florence, Alabama, forty miles south of Lawrenceburg. Fortunately, these were the days of not much in the way of entrance requirements. The next fall we both enrolled and, after commuting for a little while, moved into a government-run housing project built on the side of a bluff and inappropriately named Cherry Hills. It served as the residence for poor people and married college couples. We qualified on both counts. So we moved in, and I commuted back to Lawrenceburg on weekends to work at the furniture factory, after striking out in trying to find a part-time job in Florence.

So there I was, head of my own household—an independent man ready for anything. I went against habit and bought a six-pack of beer to celebrate my new worldliness. However, there is nothing like an unexpected demonstration of incompetence to help a young man adjust his attitude. My first one is known in Thompson folklore as "the Washateria Incident."

It started out simply enough. Since we didn't have a washing machine, Sarah assigned me the job of taking the dirty diapers to the Laundromat down the road—a place called the Washateria. It was the evening of my first major fatherly mission. I dutifully loaded the odorous bundle into the 1950 Chevy that my dad had given us and took them to the Washateria, mindful of the necessity of following the instructions that were given me. I walked in among several grizzled veterans of life's wars (other non–washing machine owners), including several women waiting for their clothes to dry. Trying to act like I knew what I was doing, I matter-of-factly put the heavy load of diapers into the machine and generously sprinkled them with the detergent that Sarah had given me.

Leaving nothing to chance, I had already obtained an ample stash of quarters for the machine. I fed them in, pushed the button, and started to look for something to read. However, I immediately noticed that I was getting strange looks. Then I heard a rather loud rattling sound, like someone had fed small particles of gravel into an air vent. I couldn't quite make it out. People were elbowing each other and nodding my way. Finally, it dawned on me. Completely unfamiliar with the machinery, I had put my entire load of dirty diapers into the big dryer, not the washing machine. Looking through the dryer window, I saw the dirty diapers tumbling in what looked like a snow blizzard of detergent, which was making the racket. Unfortunately, everyone else could see it as well.

I had a decision to make. Did I keep feeding quarters until everyone left the premises? Did I leave, go home, and try to convince Sarah that someone had stolen our dirty diapers? No, I decided to man up. When I opened the door of the dryer, the smell was almost enough to bring a man to his knees. People cleared a wide path around the area, some laughing, others just shaking their head. I quickly transferred the load to the real washing machine and hunkered down behind a newspaper. This father business was going to be tough.

My misspent youth proved to be a challenge for me academically in terms of going back and learning the basics, but my classes soon opened up a whole new world for me—ideas, history, and a host of other interesting things. After about twelve years of trying just about every other approach—including osmosis—I hit upon a new strategy: studying. I found that undertaking this innovative technique actually improved one's comprehension. It resulted in pretty fair grades right off the bat. And I had the irritating example of Sarah, who continued to get good grades with seemingly minimal effort. We found a nice middle-aged lady to stay with Tony while we were in class. I started thinking about the future. I thought of becoming an accountant. But there was a ready antidote for that thought: I took a course in accounting.

It was increasingly obvious to me during that first year that, although I didn't know how we would sustain ourselves for the six or seven years it would take, what I really wanted to be was a lawyer like Pap and A.D. I read *Yankee from Olympus*, about Oliver Wendell Holmes. I read Clarence Darrow's autobiography and was inspired by the idea of defending the little guy, taking on the government, strutting my stuff in a crowded courtroom, and weaving a spellbinding argument that would make men cheer and women weep. And I could be my own boss, independent, beholden to no one except my clearly meritorious client. These were the same thoughts that I'm sure many young people have to this day after watching Gregory Peck in *To Kill a Mockingbird*. But I was aware that neither life nor law practice was like the movies. From listening to the stories at the Lindsey gatherings at Pap's house, I already had a real solid idea about what it was like to live the life of a small-town lawyer. So at the age of eighteen I decided to become a lawyer. From then on, I never had any other thought about what I wanted to do.

However, it was clear that, even with some help from our parents, a part-time job was not going to be enough from a financial standpoint. So we decided that I would drop out of college for a semester and we would move back in with Sarah's parents in their new house and double up on the work.

The major employer for Lawrence County was the Murray Bicycle Manufacturing Plant, a company that had moved down from Murray, Ohio, and provided a major boost to our largely rural economy. It allowed men all over the county to "hurry for Murray" for an eight-hour shift and still work their farms. And the wages were the highest around. So after moving back, I got a job at Murray working the graveyard shift—11 p.m. until 7 a.m.—in Department 44 on an assembly line.

A fellow would send bicycle frames down a slide. I would grab one, place it on my machine, and drill out the sprocket area on the frame where the pedal mechanism went. Then I took it out of my machine and sent it down the next chute. My tooling machine was loud and wet, with a constant stream of water hitting the drill to keep it cool. If a heavy dose of that kind of work doesn't make a scholar out of you, nothing will. Working that shift also totally scrambles your body clock, but it freed me up most of the day to work other part-time jobs. I delivered parcels for the post office and worked weekends at my uncle Mitch's drag strip, keeping freeloaders from sneaking in across the field without paying.

Everything worked out, but a schedule like this is better as a plan than it is in its implementation. I was tired all the time and seemed to be eating breakfast three times a day. It was about 4 a.m. one morning on the assembly line, with the machines roaring and my feet wet, that it occurred to me there was a pretty large gap between my aspirations and what I was actually doing, and that when I got back to school I would embrace it with a new and unbridled enthusiasm.

And that is exactly what I did. My uncle Wayne was living in Memphis, so we decided to enroll in Memphis State University. It was a long way from home, but it seemed that that wasn't all bad either. So the next fall we packed up Tony, a few sticks of furniture, and off we went to Memphis.

It is said that the Old South meets the New South in the lobby of the Peabody Hotel—that grand old landmark two blocks from the Mississippi River—and it has been the place where cotton tycoons and politicians of all stripes have congregated for 150 years to put together big deals and drink good whiskey. In Memphis politics, racial diversity and music share the same multifaceted history to produce one of the most interesting places on earth. Memphis is the commercial home of the delta blues, as well as W. C. Handy, B. B. King, Elvis Presley, and Jerry Lee Lewis. Across town another young man by the name of Isaac Hayes, one day younger than I was, was laying the groundwork for his own legendary status. Walking down Beale Street and then along the Mississippi River, these two Lawrenceburg kids felt the excitement not only of being on our own, but of taking in a rich, historical, and different place that was far bigger than anything else we had experienced.

But practical considerations had to be dealt with. We rented a little house on Mynders Avenue just a couple of blocks from campus, across the street from a fraternity house. There was a swing in the backyard for Tony, and we were a couple of blocks from both the Church of Christ and a public library. The only downside besides the fraternity noise was the $65 a month we were paying in rent. It was entirely too steep. But soon I had a sales job, after classes, at Lowery's, a mom-and-pop children's shoe store. Sarah had a 7 a.m. class. She would walk to class, and I would dress Tony and we would get in the car and drive to the campus. I'd meet Sarah, get out of the car to go to my 8 a.m. class, and she would get in and drive home with Tony. At Lowery's, amid the squawking kids and the flustered mothers, I was learning to deal with people instead of heavy machinery or stacks of lumber. Sarah put together whatever she had for my lunch bag each day, and I got to experience different combinations I had never thought about, such as peanut butter and jelly on rye.

Money was going to get tighter, but for a happy reason: the birth of our little girl, Ruth Elizabeth, or "Betsy" as we called her. She was a sweet little thing with reddish auburn hair that soon developed into ringlets. We had to find some new housing that would meet the needs of our shrinking pocketbooks.

What I was finding, as I settled into a stable, responsible life of husband and father, was that my hard work and focus, along with Sarah's, could create opportunities, and sometimes good things just happened. For example, just when we needed more-affordable housing, a vacancy opened up in "Vet's Village," the married-student housing on campus. Built decades earlier with little more than plywood for returning vets, they were one- and two-bedroom apartments with three apartments to a building. The joke was that you could sneeze in the apartment at one end of the building and be heard on the other. But they were $35 a month, including utilities, and it was on campus. That allowed us to develop the routine that we followed for the rest of our time in Memphis: Sarah and I would schedule our classes so that we could alternate. She would go to class and I would stay at home with the kids, and then I would go to class while she was at home. Then, in the late afternoon, I would go to work until 9 o'clock, at which time I would return and we would have dinner.

For the first time since she had been married, my mom took a part-time job out of the house. She became a bookkeeper at an appliance store to help us out.

My daddy may have been a "car man," but I was showing an affinity for shoes. Soon, I had moved from the kiddie set at Lowery's to Chamberlin's and Lowenstein's East, where I sold ladies' shoes. Eventually, I moved to Bond's Men's

Store. However, before I started selling men's suits I had to buy one, since I didn't have one at the time. I had one gray sports coat, which actually belonged to my dad. It was a little short, but I didn't have much call to wear it. So my first sale at Bond's was to myself. It was the easiest sale I'd ever made.

Just What the
World Needs . . .

A LOT OF CHANGES were taking place, many of them within me. School was taking me to places that I had never been before. I felt like I'd been thrown in the lake and was discovering I knew how to swim. In fact, I loved the water. The professors, the subjects, the library books I checked out for extra reading, all presented me with a vast array of new ideas and questions that sparked my imagination and made me hungry for more. In other words, college was doing for me exactly what it was supposed to do. Never far from my mind was what was enabling this transformation: If I had been a single guy living in that frat house on Mynders Street, the only serious ideas I would have had could have fit in a thimble with room left over. And they would have had nothing to do with Socrates or Plato unless they sold beer or wore skirts.

I was drawn to the subjects of philosophy and political science, even serving as president of the Philosophy Club. I suppose imprecise subjects where all ideas are on the table were natural choices for a guy who had still not quite mastered the multiplication tables. How do we know what we know? Is it through our experience or our senses, which can deceive us, or do humans inherently know certain things? Are ethics and morality objective or subjective? I was especially interested in the interrelation of the two subjects and how powerful ideas precede political movements—how the supposed nonpolitical conclusions of philosophers like some of the Greeks, Locke, Hegel, and Bentham form the basis of political movements for years, even centuries thereafter. Philosophy had to do with the purpose and nature of man. It seemed to me that once you resolved those questions in your mind, then your politics are pretty well defined for you.

I read all I could get my hands on about the French Revolution. The French Revolution served as the opening salvo—starting with Edmund Burke and Jean-Jacques Rousseau—in a war of ideas about the nature of man that has been fought ever since. Rousseau viewed man as essentially innocent, corrupted by society, and if unfettered, he would live happily ever after. He supported the Revolution, in spite of all its excesses, as a good thing that would serve as a beneficial example for mankind. Burke believed that man tended to err and would engage in excesses if unrestrained by tradition, authority, and God. He predicted that the Revolution would lead to more bloodshed and misery than good. To me, Burke won the first philosophical battle between liberalism and conservatism. However, my own political views were developing rather slowly.

I didn't quite yet see how all of this translated into the politics of the day. Back home when someone would ask me what my major was in college and I would say philosophy, I could invariably tell they were thinking: "What in the heck is he going to do with that?" So I would add with a straight face, "I am planning on coming back to Lawrenceburg and opening up a little philosophy shop on the square." Some would laugh, and some said they thought that it would be a good idea.

For me—with all that I learned from my parents around the dinner table and my long talks with the Lindsey men—the basic political issue was "What is the proper role of government?" I was affected by countervailing factors. There was the Scotch-Irish Southern part of me that didn't want anybody telling me what to do—especially the government (although I didn't mind taking government school loans). I saw myself as independent (even if I wasn't). Mainly, I saw myself not as I was—on the bottom rung of the economic ladder—but as the man I planned to be. There was simply not one of my acquaintances who had worked hard and behaved himself who wasn't doing pretty well.

Dad was a good example of that. As I was growing up, my folks had very little tolerance for people who were "lazy and no-'count" (with the possible exception of myself). The first question upon hearing of a good girl's impending marriage was "Is he a hard worker?" If so, then morals and character were pretty well assumed. And identifying with "the little man" was part of my heritage. Ma and Pa Thompson had a little bust of Franklin Roosevelt on the "whatnot shelf" in their living room. Memories of the Great Depression never completely left them—and never left my mom and dad, for that matter.

In my various jobs I had never been particularly respectful of authority. Even at my in-laws' factory I had a run-in with the foreman who didn't like the way I was stacking lumber and made what I thought were some unnecessary comments about it. If you were a "working man" you understood your position, but nobody that I knew would put up with disparaging comments even from his boss. None of this had translated into any particular sympathy for a political party. Oscar had actually taken me with him to an organizing meeting of the Lawrence County Democratic Party a year or so earlier.

On November 22, 1963, I was walking home from class when I heard the news that President Kennedy had been assassinated. Like everyone else I was shocked and dismayed. Not knowing anything else to do, I went to the office of the head of the Political Science Department, Dr. Edwin Buell, whom I respected and who taught two of my classes. Others were also gathered there. We all had the need to share this terrible experience and talk about it. There was an immediate and substantial sentiment that right-wing rhetoric had instigated this tragedy. Dr. Buell pointed out that even if that was true, the conservative leader, Barry Goldwater, could not be blamed for such talk.

I remember being pleasantly surprised by the professor's reaction. Earlier that year, we were required to do a book report. I chose *The Road to Serfdom* by F. A. Hayek, a conservative classic that demonstrated the folly of centralized economic planning and the loss of freedom that comes from it. Dr. Buell approved the selection, but only if I would incorporate the work of a Hayek critic, Herman Finer's *The Road to Reaction*. I was quite certain that no other student was being asked to provide "balance" in his book report. These two incidents demonstrated to me that the professor was basically a fair-minded man but when it came to ideology he simply couldn't let the conservative viewpoint go unchallenged.

Sarah's folks had given us a little portable TV for Christmas, and we watched in anguish along with the rest of the nation as President Kennedy's little boy, not much older than Tony, saluted as the horse-drawn carriage carrying his daddy's coffin rolled by. I had no strong feelings one way or the other about Kennedy as a president, but the human tragedy of those few days focused me intensely on the fragility of life and the threat of harm out there in the real world. I watched President Johnson's touching speech after his swearing-in. I took note of his Texas accent and his seeming sincerity. "Maybe this fellow will keep me in the Democratic Party," I thought.

Youth and deadlines allowed me to refocus quickly. Not to mention a constant strain of life's inevitable trials, such as everyone in the family coming down with intestinal flu at the same time, or having the car stolen at work one night with our Christmas packages in the trunk (thoughtfully, I left the key in the ignition, so the thieves could have a merrier holiday) and walking home miles in the snow. I developed my sales and diplomatic skills, as I was able to fit quite a few women with size 9 feet into size 7½ shoes, at their insistence. There is a whole generation of ladies out there with crippled feet, and I did my part. "Looks good to me, ma'am."

The grades kept improving—pretty much all A's and B's. Although I could have gone to several law schools after three years of college, I wanted to take a shot at getting into Vanderbilt, which required a college degree. Sarah had already graduated, and we decided that we would stay at Memphis straight through the summer of 1964 to make up for the semester that I had lost and get my degree. One day I received a call from Dr. Buell. He told me that Tulane Law School gave a full-tuition scholarship to a Memphis State political science student, and he had selected me to be the recipient. I was ecstatic. But I still wanted to go to Vanderbilt. Not only was it in Tennessee, but Vanderbilt had long represented achievement that I, until recently, considered to be way beyond my reach—both scholastically and financially.

I applied to Vanderbilt with a generous letter of recommendation from an unlikely source—Mrs. Buckner, the teacher who led the effort to stop my "Most Athletic" designation as a high school junior. A Vanderbilt graduate, she'd kept up with my efforts since that time (easy to do in a small town) and was more than happy to help me with regard to Vanderbilt Law School. She was a significant reminder of a simple but powerful lesson: When you don't do well, bad things tend to happen to you. And when you try to do your best, you often get lucky. Soon we received the word we had been waiting for. I had been accepted into Vanderbilt Law School with a half-tuition scholarship. That was it. We would make up the difference in loans and work.

There was just one final hurdle to overcome during my final semester: a liberal professor. Many conservative students across the country know what I am talking about.

By my senior year, I had increasingly grown enamored of conservative thinking, and when it became apparent that Barry Goldwater was going to be the Republican nominee for president, I read his little book, *The Conscience of a Conservative,* and it had a powerful impact on me. It carried a message of individualism and freedom. It laid out the ways in which government was growing too big and stifling individual initiative. His words rang true to me. They placed into focus and provided a landing place for my many scattered political thoughts. Also, they were being presented by what appeared to be a somewhat cantankerous straight shooter with an accent that could just as well come from the hills of Tennessee as the desert in Arizona. Goldwater was not your average politician. He and his thinking inspired me. I even liked the fact that the experts said he couldn't win the presidency. It all appealed to my youthful idealism.

Although my friends and family had conservative viewpoints, the Republican Party had little standing in the South; everyone still seemed to be trying to reconcile their values with the policies of the Democratic Party. But it's a reconciliation that I could not make. So although my state, my country, and my dad, along with most of the Lindseys, were Democratic, I decided I was going to be a Republican. Pap is the only Republican I had really known, and by this time he had passed away. So in the beginning it was just Barry and me. Besides, I wasn't smoking pot or demonstrating in the street, and this allowed me to be a rebel too, in my own way.

So with the confidence of a general with no army behind him, I would sit in my liberal professor's history course and take it all in. He would periodically stop reading his lecture notes long enough to launch into an anti-U.S. diatribe. By this time, I was reading anything I could get my hands on that was political, and I discovered that he was getting a lot of his material from *The New Republic,* the main liberal magazine of the day. I, on the other hand, was getting rebuttal material from William F. Buckley's *National Review.* It made for a combustible combination. I would raise my hand and beg to disagree with him on his assertions, rebutting his talking points with my own.

One day the subject was the downtrodden condition of

some little country and how their plight was the fault of the good old U.S. of A. You might say I hit a nerve that day, because in the middle of our little back-and-forth he picked up his papers and marched out of the class, stopping at the door to say, "Be careful, Mr. Thompson, you are going to wake up with your head missing some morning." From the hand of some peasant, I presumed. Being quick on the up-take, I immediately concluded that he was not happy with me—on a personal basis. Actually, my thought was more along the lines of "Holy ——." I could imagine an F on my final transcript and a reevaluation by Vanderbilt. After a restless night, I went to the dean of students and told him what had happened and that I didn't deserve this impending doom. He was noncommittal. But when the grades came out, I received a B in the class. And I still had my head . . . and a future in Nashville as a law student.

Our two and a half years in Memphis was a special time in our lives. Betsy had been born. We had proven to ourselves that in fact we could do the things we had set out to do. But it was also bittersweet in some ways. The fact is that I cannot remember the name of one person I graduated with. We simply did not spend any time at all on campus except when we were having class. Even though the trade-offs made it more than worth it, we clearly missed out on some relation-ships that could have lasted a lifetime. I had started keeping a journal while in Memphis. With rare exceptions I would set out the day's happenings and my observations on them and the world at night before I went to bed. I kept this up for seven or eight years until I lost the journals, apparently in one of our many moves. But many times I have thought about the first entry I made in that journal one night at home in Memphis. I remember starting out with a statement that was somewhat defensive because I had never considered the keeping of a "diary" to be a very manly thing to do. Therefore, I noted that I was going to call it a journal instead of a diary and that I was keeping this journal because after I had become a United States senator, perhaps future generations of Thompsons would be interested in my early years. It was totally tongue in cheek—meant to be humorous.

It was obvious from the beginning at Vanderbilt Law School that we were not in Lawrenceburg anymore. My fellow students were mostly from the best schools in the country and at the top of their class. However, not for the last time, I applied a surefire recipe for success. I had put myself in a position where I had no choice but to succeed. The alternative was too grave to consider (including having to get a real job).

Before long, our family had settled into a routine that would see us through law school—one that we were familiar with, including Sarah becoming pregnant again. In 1965, we had a handsome baby boy to the delight of us all, although I can imagine our families were wondering just how large our household was going to become before I started drawing a paycheck. We named our baby Daniel after Sarah's uncle A.D., and while he was basically healthy and strong, he provided us with the first real terror of our parenthood. He started having seizures, and under doctor's orders we would lay him on the floor and sponge him with water until he revived. It seemed like forever as he lay there with his eyes rolled back. Soon these episodes subsided without lasting effects. (He, like Tony, is a good, successful guy and lives with his wonderful family in Nashville.) But I do believe these experiences had lasting effects on Sarah and me. We had never truly recognized how lucky we had been until then.

People decide to go to law school for a lot of different reasons. Some want to use their legal knowledge to save the world (not that many, really, but some), some want to go to Wall Street and get filthy rich, and some consider it to be a convenient landing pad while they decide what they want to do when they grow up, usually with Daddy's help. Me, I still wanted to walk into a courtroom and show them who was boss. I felt that the curriculum did not serve my purpose terribly well. With the exception of one class on courtroom procedure, there was nothing very practical about it. We followed the case law method, immersing ourselves in various arcane appellate court decisions, not to learn the law but to learn how to dissect and analyze the legal opinion in the case under consideration. A phrase was heard often: "We're not here to teach you the law. We're here to teach you how to think." Of course, anyone as smart as we thought we were was of the firm opinion that they already knew how to think. We "thought" that this might be a waste of time. That was until we received our first round of grades, at which point many shattered egos were heard to say that they "thought" they needed a beer.

It also occurred to me that a fellow like myself who had majored in philosophy shouldn't squawk too much about not being taught enough that was practical. Grade shock, classroom humiliation, and onerous assignments were, of course, part of an old law-school tradition to break us down. Sometimes I felt the plan was definitely working. I knew that I was—at school, at home, and as a night clerk at a local motel. But I knew that Sarah was working as hard and doing as much or more. She was teaching high school English. In the morning, the babysitter would arrive and Sarah would leave to teach. Tony and I would get picked up by my law school buddy, Howard Liebengood, then we'd drop Tony off at school and go to class. When Sarah got out of school, she would pick me up and I would take her home and leave for my job at the motel. When I would get home, she would be in bed. Many days the only chance we had to talk was when she was taking me to work.

Howard and I had hit it off immediately. He was a funny, outgoing guy with a ready smile whom everybody liked. He was a conservative and a Hoosier, from Plymouth, Indiana, and married to a sweet, smart girl, Deana, who also taught school. We became friends for life.

Meanwhile, I was still learning life's little lessons. Much like in college, my grades steadily improved as I settled into my various tasks. But unlike a lot of my classmates, I had to work hard for everything I achieved. I had a setback my first semester, when my grade point average dropped below the B I had to retain for my partial scholarship. The school withdrew it. I was a little upset and of the opinion that the school was hasty in their decision. Therefore, I punished them by obstinately refusing to reapply for my scholarship money when my grades qualified me again. During my second year, we learned that there was a new scholarship available for someone in our class, and it was based totally upon need. You can guess who I thought would be a worthy recipient. Several of my classmates told me that they expected me to get it. They gave it instead to a judge's son. The chip on my shoulder wasn't getting any smaller. I was getting a little tired of God's apparent attempt to motivate me through the dumb actions of human intermediaries. But I guess it was still working. I won Best Oral Argument in the moot court competition and was selected for the three-person national moot court team the next year. But it didn't pay any money.

After my second year of law school, we moved back to Lawrenceburg for the summer. A.D. had given me the opportunity to clerk in his office. He practiced solo, in the same office where he and Pap had lawyered for many years. It was upstairs in an old building on the square. After climbing the stairs, the first thing one noticed was that the hallway was lit by a single lightbulb hanging from the ceiling—sort of a *Psycho* effect, but with Southern charm. It led to a two-room office filled with the aroma of old books and tobacco. After many years of bachelorhood, A.D. remarried, and "Miss Helen" did the secretarial work in the front room, where I hung out, along with a fairly steady stream of local politicians and A.D.'s friends and cronies, and shot the breeze. In the unlikely event that an actual paying client would come by, he would be taken to the back room for a modicum of privacy.

Although the space was a little cramped, it was the place of many happy hours for me, spent smoking my pipe and searching for obscure precedents that would deal a devastating blow to our local legal opponents in the case at hand: a property dispute, a divorce, or the never-ending quest to determine who got to the intersection first.

The level of regular legal traffic in A.D.'s office probably would not have justified my clerkship. But this summer was different. In 1966, Lawrenceburg was in the middle of labor turmoil the likes of which we had never seen before. The Teamsters Union had decided to make an all-out effort to unionize the Murray Bicycle Plant, my former employer, as well as some smaller firms, including the Lindsey's furniture plant.

Employee elections had been conducted and the union was voted down, but that was just the beginning of the fight. The Teamsters filed unfair-labor-practice charges against the companies, accusing them of intimidation and a raft of other offenses. For a little company like Lindsey's the fines and penalties, not to mention the effects of losing a new election, would have been disastrous. Ed and Oscar had started in the business as teenagers and worked day and night to build it up. They provided jobs to mostly country folks, and paid wages that would seem small to most outside observers but were not bad by local standards. They especially didn't like being told that they couldn't talk to their own employees about what they thought was in the best interest of them and the plant. A lot was at stake. Although the factory had provided Ed's and Oscar's families with pretty good livings, the profit margins were small. Fortunately for them, they had access to the most high-powered legal team in those parts— A.D. and me. There was just one problem. A.D. knew nothing about labor law . . . and I knew even less. What we did know was that the hearing examiner for the National Labor Relations Board had taken testimony and found against Lindsey's and the case was on appeal to the NLRB. Fortunately, the appeal was pretty much a fact-based exercise. A.D. and I spent hour after hour going through transcripts of the hearing, preparing our brief to the NLRB.

I had never seen A.D. work before. He was brilliant. During World War II, he had worked in New York as a military investigator of some sort. He never talked much about it, but occasionally he would reminisce about his days in New York as he wistfully recalled them. He was a big fan of Thomas

Wolfe and was one of the most well-read guys in the area. He simply got tired of all of it and came home to the little town to practice law with Pap. He knew the trade-offs and he loved what he was doing, but his experiences had left him a bit more cosmopolitan than he was willing to acknowledge. The NLRB also challenged him as the local legal fare never had before.

There were union fights, skirmishes, and lawsuits filed almost every other day that summer, and many Murray hearings were held at the courthouse. Observing the large team of Murray lawyers in from Atlanta, it occurred to me at the time that they were indeed specialists but they were no smarter than A.D. He was doing the same kind of work and was a heck of a lot cheaper. My guess is that he never received a dime. The Lindseys just did things for one another.

While these battles were being fought out in the courts and before the NLRB, an uglier side of the conflict was being played out in the streets and at the factory gates. The Teamsters' main goal was to get new elections for union recognition at the factories. While the legal efforts were pending, they sent "business agents" from Nashville to organize and rabble-rouse. Teamster sympathizers left their jobs and started congregating at the factory gate at Murray to hassle nonstriking workers and stop them from going to work. Hell broke loose. Trying to interfere with a man's livelihood, especially when done by outsiders, was not something to be tolerated by the average Lawrence Countian. Fights broke out in twos and threes, and then in larger numbers. The local chief of police was hospitalized. Gunshots were heard in the distance. At Lindsey's they threw bricks through the front-office window and injured Sarah's mother. However, the main action was at Murray, and it was getting worse. The police department called for volunteers. I borrowed a pistol from a friend of mine and showed up at the police station, where several of us were "deputized." The city fathers established a system whereby the fire station siren would be activated when the thugs showed up, usually at the Murray gate during the change in shifts. Often it was brother against brother and father against son. Each side was armed, untrained, without leadership, and mad as hell—all of the ingredients for a major disaster. One night the siren went off and we headed for Murray. Strikers were pelting cars with rocks as they were going through the factory gate. After a lot of shoving, cussing, and threatening, things finally calmed down. This scene was repeated a few times until it was obvious to the union organizers that we outnumbered them and would not back off. I have no idea what I or any of the rest of the crowd would have done if real violence had broken out. Miraculously, no one was killed.

Just as miraculously, the NLRB overturned the hearing examiner in the Lindsey case. We had won. The result of it all was that neither Lindsey's nor Murray was unionized. Mainly, it was due not to the legalities of the matter, but because most of the workers simply chose not to unionize.

They felt they could deal with management better themselves. It had worked so far. And they, for sure, were against allowing a bunch of outsiders and roughnecks to tell them what to do.

For me it was a story about the Lindseys as much as anything else. They had stuck it out and were fortunate enough to have a good lawyer in the family. Their closeness and even clannishness made it one for all and all for one, allowing them to afford to fight. My understanding was that a year or two later, when Oscar and Ed made some office furniture for A.D. and a desk for me, it was largely in payment to A.D. for what he had done. It cost far less than what they would have had to pay lawyers from Atlanta, but it meant a lot to A.D. and to me.

When you are doing manual labor, whether it's digging a ditch or working at an assembly line, you get to see humanity with its clothes off. Sometimes it's not a pretty picture. Sometimes it is. In other words, it's pretty much the same as in a law office or a business, but without the pretention.

The lessons I learned that summer solidified some feelings I had. For one thing, I saw that good old boys coming in off the farms can't be counted on by the activists to line up on the left because of class resentment. The working men whom I had encountered liked to think for themselves and, unless personally disrespected, were not naturally resentful of "the man." And what made it that way was not so much that they were delighted with where they were at any particular moment in their life but their belief that they could and would do better tomorrow.

I knew where people like my folks and the Lindseys had come from. I knew of the economic transition that they had made while all the time keeping their families together and making them stronger. Since the beginning of our country, we have been a nation of dreamers and hard workers, and we've encouraged and rewarded them. We seldom envy achievers because we know that we are free to take our own shot at success. Even though most of my working buddies did not have the prospects that I did, for all of us it was not as much about yesterday or today as it was about tomorrow. What we did with it was, largely, up to us.

Back in law school for my final year, I had to smile when asked what I had done on my summer vacation. I wanted to say, "Well, I won my first case, carried a gun, and busted a strike." But I wasn't sure how well that would have gone over—or whether it would be believed, for that matter.

Mitch

ONE IS NEVER PREPARED when serious illness strikes a member of the family, especially when it's sudden and the victim has always been strong and carefree. Uncle Mitch was his usual jaunty self when he told us, "Hodgkin's disease, ever heard of it?" I hadn't heard of it, but I could tell that Dad and the others had from their solemn demeanor. It was a mean form of cancer, and in the early 1960s it was usually a death sentence. Mitch proceeded with chemotherapy treatments the way he approached everything else—undaunted. Once, a few years earlier, when he was scheduled to have a minor surgical procedure, he said matter-of-factly, "Surgery doesn't bother me any more than if they were cutting a piece of meat." Even accounting for a certain amount of hyperbole, it was clear that he meant it. That contrasted with a view that I had heard Dad express: "Minor surgery is surgery that someone else is having."

Soon it was obvious that Mitch was in serious trouble.

When I was in Lawrenceburg home from law school and would go to visit him, he was always deathly sick from the chemotherapy and hardly able to talk. He would throw up continually. This strong man began to waste away before our eyes. He spent his final days in the hospital. Dad was having a hard time going into his room. Once robust and over six feet tall, Mitch had become grotesquely emaciated. There was nothing more that could be done for him. I would go into his hospital room from time to time as the designated family member. I was in the room the night he finally died, fighting for every breath.

Mitch's death vividly returned to me in the fall of 2004. I had married Jeri Kehn in 2002 and left the Senate in January of the next year. Jeri and I had a beautiful, healthy one-year-old daughter, Hayden. I had resumed my acting career. (Having been in law and politics, some might say, I'd never left it.)

In late 2001, after I had announced that I was not going to run for reelection to the Senate, I received a call from Dick Wolf, the creator and producer of *Law & Order*. At the time, the show was about to tie *Gunsmoke* as the longest-running dramatic TV series in the history of television. The show had made Dick Wolf a legend. Actually, I had never seen an episode of *Law & Order,* although Jeri was a big fan.

Dick said he wanted to talk to me about an idea he had—me playing the district attorney on *Law & Order*. It was totally out of the blue. I asked him if the show was set in New

York, and he confirmed that it was. I asked him if he thought that the audience might catch on that maybe I hadn't exactly grown up in the Bronx. They had fixed that, he said— Southerner in big law firm moves to New York after September 11 and wants to do public service. Then I wondered if it was going to be another deal where the lone Southerner was going to be portrayed in a not very flattering light (usually with a phony accent). Dick assured me that he had something else in mind. My DA would actually get to articulate a conservative point of view on occasion without coming off as a Neanderthal—a TV rarity indeed. Although I had minor run-ins with a few of the writers from time to time, Dick's assurances panned out.

So I was happy, fit, and looking to the future as always, even getting back to working out on a regular basis. For insurance purposes, the actors always had to get a physical examination before each season's shoot. They didn't want an actor keeling over in the middle of a workweek and costing them a lot of money. I always looked upon this perfunctory examination as a nuisance. It was filling out paperwork more than anything else. During the exam this time, the studio's doctor felt a small lump in my neck. Calling on my own medical "expertise," I thought it was probably just a swollen gland. He agreed that that could be the case but said that I ought to get it looked at more closely. Otherwise, I checked out fine. I walked out of his office proud of the fact that my blood pressure was, as always, perfect.

I checked on the lump from time to time when I was shaving, expecting it to disappear. When it didn't, at Jeri's urging, I had my regular doctor take a look at it. He said that in order to be on the safe side he was going to send me to a specialist who would aspirate the lump—that is, stick a needle in it and draw out enough tissue to put it under a microscope. In a few days the results came back—negative. It was just as I thought. Nothing to worry about. So I put it out of my mind.

However, over the next several weeks I kept noticing that the small lump still presented itself. A small dose of common sense kicked in. It finally dawned on me that it is not normal for a man to be walking around the rest of his life with a lump in his neck if there was no reason for it. Through another doctor friend of mine, I arranged for an examination with a specialist in Boston, who put me through a series of tests and basically told me that he could not make a conclusive diagnosis. This situation now really began to get my attention. I arranged to be seen by the doctors at Sloan-Kettering, which had nationally renowned cancer specialists. There they explained the possibilities in fuller detail, essentially from nothing to malignancy. I noted that the lump hadn't gotten any larger. But that fact didn't seem to impress them much. They said that the only way they could tell for sure was by doing a biopsy. I told them, "Let's get it done." I still assumed that the doctors were just being very careful in laying out the worst possibility, but it was time that I knew exactly what was going on. Of course, this biopsy sounded like full-fledged surgery to me—the operating room and being put to sleep while they cut into my neck. I thought of Dad's definition of minor surgery.

The day before the procedure, Jeri and I flew to New York. After we checked into the hotel, we walked out into crowded streets of Christmas shoppers. It was freezing cold, but it was a glorious day. To me, the air smelled sweet, the people were friendly, and every block was a new adventure. We lingered in a little store on a side street that sold nothing but beautiful miniature carousels and bought one for Hayden. I encouraged Jeri to try on some outrageously expensive coats on Fifth Avenue, which she thoughtfully declined to purchase. I tried on a Russian fur hat as a joke, and at Jeri's insistence wound up buying it and wearing it the rest of the trip. What a day. I was the one who wound up with the fur.

Of course, what was happening had more to do with what was going on inside me than it did with the reality around me. Even the outside possibility of bad news had heightened a dormant sensitivity to what I otherwise would have considered to be mundane. Suddenly, everything in life had become precious.

The operation went off without a hitch, and several days later the results of the biopsy were in. Jeri, Hayden, and I were in the final stages of packing to leave for Nashville for the Christmas holidays with Mom and the rest of the family when I received the call. No malignancy. Home free. Jeri and I had kept everything about my health issue secret, and a few days later at a family gathering we told them about the scare and the good news we had received. It was a great Christmas, to say the least. I didn't realize that the story was not over.

About ten days later, after we returned from the Christmas holiday, I was driving across the Roosevelt Bridge to our home in Virginia when my cell phone rang. It was the doctor from Sloan-Kettering. They had done some further testing. As I understood it, it was a more sophisticated level of genetic and molecular testing. These further tests revealed that their original opinion had been wrong. The biopsy indicated malignancy after all.

A few days later, I was sitting in the doctor's office in New York listening to the details. I had what they called non-Hodgkin's lymphoma, and indeed it was a form of cancer. However, there are different types of this disease. Mine was the slow-growing indolent kind, which of course is good, although incurable in that you cannot eradicate it forever. But, through treatment, you can hope to keep it in remission for long periods, maybe even indefinitely. When and if it reoccurs, you can treat it again and buy another chunk of time. These are statistical generalities, of course, partly dependent on one's response to the treatment. Hodgkin's disease, which Mitch had died from, is a type of lymphoma. To add to the irony, nowadays Hodgkin's is considered to be curable. My former colleague, Arlen Specter, the senator from Pennsylvania, had Hodgkin's disease in 2007 and, after treatment, is going strong at the age of seventy-nine. Strong enough, in fact, to switch parties and run for another six-year term as a Democrat. (Maybe it was the treatment that did that to him.)

No matter how much "good news" is connected with it, once you hear the C word, you are never quite the same. You know from that day forward that there is a stranger out-side your door and you simply have to do everything you can to keep him from coming in. I went through all the range of emotions that one might expect. Considering my age, I kept calculating how many years it would be before Hayden fin-ished high school, college, got married, and so on. I can honestly say that there was little self-pity. Objectively, I knew that in many ways I had already lived several lives, and I had daily reminders of the young people losing their lives in Iraq before ever even knowing their children. Then again, no-body is really objective at a time like this.

I suppose I like to think that I am very much a Thompson in a way that served me well during this period of time. When I was growing up, the tougher things got, the better Dad got. I think this was true with regard to a lot of things in his life, but, naturally, I noticed it the most when it per-tained to me. My earliest memory is when, as a child, I was being wheeled into the operating room to have my tonsils removed, scared to death. I remember Dad's calm as he assured me that he was going to perform the operation, the one idea that he knew would calm me down. When I accidentally pushed the end of a crochet hook deep into my finger, he kept me from panicking while he worked it out. When I broke my arm in the second grade, they had to remove the cast while I was still in the doctor's office and put the bones back in place again. When, while horsing around, I broke the window at a local restaurant. When I had to tell him and Mom that I was going to get married, having just turned seventeen. When misfortune hit, whether by accident or my own actions, he was a pillar of strength and understanding. It was the way he dealt with me, and it was the way that he dealt with other people. He was simply a fellow who could be relied upon. When I became an adult, I realized that now it was my turn to exhibit those same traits. It was something that he gave to me that neither college degrees nor wealth could buy. I felt it every time things got a little tough. The key is not always to live up to the standards that are set for you but that you always try. It's like what someone said about a conscience: It doesn't keep you from engaging in bad behavior, it just makes it so you can't enjoy it nearly as much. And I didn't enjoy it very much when I did not live up to Dad's standards. My uncle Mitch, with a lot more swagger, fit the same mold.

The more I was learning about my condition, the better I felt about it. There was a drug, Rituxan, that had become available just five years earlier that was approved for my condition. I soon began my treatment at the Lombardi Cancer Center at the Georgetown Hospital in Washington, under the care of Dr. Bruce Cheson. The medicine was administered intravenously for a couple of hours at a time. Although I was told that the side effects were nothing like chemotherapy's, I was prepared for the worst. But, surprisingly, there were no aftereffects at all. None. I would receive a treatment, get unhooked, and go on about my business as if nothing had happened. After a few intermittent CT scans and MRIs, I was pronounced to be in total remission. My last treatment was in 2005, and I now go in for a checkup every six months or so. From the very beginning I have not had one sick day. I have every reason to believe, with just what is available in today's medicine, that I can live a normal life span—in large part due to a drug that was not available until a few years ago.

The disease from which Mitch had died a young and agonizing death was not exactly what I had, but it was pretty doggone close, and today people with exactly what Mitch had are living happy lives in remission. Countless numbers of people, including children, have died over the centuries from diseases that are treatable or manageable today. This is in large part due to the miracle of modern medicine. I recall the many times I sat on the Senate floor and listened to colleagues who would rail against the "big drug companies" and their profits, disregarding the billions of dollars spent and the years that pass before a new drug can be brought to the market. Not only did I have reason to appreciate modern medicine for my condition, but it is also probably keeping my mother alive. What kind of price tag should we put on that? One hopes the answer will continue to be provided by America's free market and not a government that fixes prices and rations health care in order to contain costs. If that happens, the research and development simply won't be there. We should help those who can't afford modern medicine, but we should never slow down its development.

As usual, I am reminded of something that Dad said. It's kind of a gruesome recollection in some respects, but Dad loved his cigarettes. He had been smoking since he was old enough to walk. One day, when he heard some of his buddies complain that the price of cigarettes had gone up again, he replied, "Boys, they're just getting up close to what they're worth." That's the way I feel about these drugs. I know that Mitch would have agreed with me.

Finally,
a Country Lawyer

URING OUR THIRD and last year of law school, the
tension rose among us would-be lawyers as to where
we were going to be employed upon graduation. I have
since come to the realization that your first job out of school
is probably one of the least important occurrences in your
life, at least from a career standpoint. Whatever it turns out
to be, you probably won't do it for very long. New grads,
bright-eyed but inexperienced in anything but school, develop in different ways. In the case of law grads, some lose
interest in the law altogether once they realize that, in addition to being an interesting profession, it is the way they are
going to have to make their living. Some of the best students
get hired by the best and largest law firms in the nation,
which consign them to a back room researching, writing
memos, and becoming the base of the firm pyramid, which
is designed to achieve large profit margins for the partners at
the top. Sometime during that first year, the young lawyer

realizes that it ain't the kind of law work that they make movies about.

For many, the first job out of law school is the beginning of a career of job-hopping from firm to firm and in and out of government—a pattern that lasts a lifetime. Staying in one place with one firm for an extended period of time is pretty much a thing of the past. And so is the idealism of many young lawyers. The profession has changed over the years. As I was coming out of school, it was clear that we were becoming a much more transient and commercialized society and the legal profession, after standing apart as a pure profession for a couple of centuries, was becoming very much a part of the society around it. The notion of going into law not to become wealthy, but because of the status, independence, and respect it brought, was rapidly becoming a quaint notion. Journalism and the legal profession are the only two jobs in America directly protected by Constitutional amendments—the First and the Sixth. That comes with special responsibilities, including not being, primarily, a commercial enterprise. Neither profession has fully lived up to that responsibility. I longed for the "good old days," at least as I perceived them. But in 1967 my focus was much narrower and probably more intense than most—a focus befitting a twenty-five-year-old married man with three children. I just wanted a job.

My uncertainty was cut short when I received a letter

from A.D. offering me a job with him. He was prepared to double the size of his office—from one to two. The firm would be called Lindsey and Thompson, and I would start out at $50 per week until I could develop my own clients. Sarah and I looked at each other and smiled. We knew we were going home. I would be a small fish in a small pond, with every confidence I could grow faster than the pond.

So the table had been set for me. I was going back to my hometown to do the only thing I ever wanted to do—be a country lawyer.

It turned out that practicing law in Lawrenceburg in the 1960s was a lot like it was in *To Kill a Mockingbird,* but without anyone who looked like Atticus Finch. The pace of the practice was pretty well demonstrated by a young lawyer who excitedly told some of the older heads having coffee one day, "I had a great week last week. I got a $100 case and a couple of small ones."

However, when you've been chomping at the bit to practice law, as I had been for several years, nothing is too small to stir a young barrister's juices. I couldn't wait—so I didn't.

A.D. had bought a little one-story frame house about a block and a half from the courthouse and turned it into our offices. We had "Lindsey and Thompson" painted on the door in gold leaf. And at the factory, Oscar and Ed had made a desk for me and a library table with legs on it from an old piano. I called them the best-looking legs in town. After screwing in a light fixture one day, I had left a screwdriver sitting on our new table. Uncle Robert walked in, took a look at it, and said, "Ah-ha, a tool of the trade."

I started sitting in on meetings with A.D. and his clients, helping out where I could and even voicing an opinion or two. Actually, I became quite involved in some of the cases in the office. The only problem was . . . I wasn't a lawyer. As I recall, it took a couple of months from the time we took our bar examination until we heard the results. It seemed like the wait was a lifetime. I had studied for the bar in a cold sweat—day and night. The thought of not passing the bar with the responsibilities I had and all that awaited me was terrifying. With me sitting behind my new desk with my name on the door and Sarah, my family, and her family close by, it seemed like Western civilization was waiting to see my bar results. My thoughts kept drifting back to "What if I don't pass?" My smart-aleck comments during my college days about the philosophy shop on the square didn't seem so funny now. Finally, the word was circulating that the bar results would appear in the next Sunday's edition of the *Nashville Tennessean*. The papers would come on early Sunday morning and be delivered to a little shack there in Lawrenceburg for distribution by the paperboys. On the following Sunday at about 3 a.m., I was waiting when the papers arrived. We cut a batch open, and sure enough my name was on the list. I had passed. I sat down on another stack of papers and read the list over and over again. Each time my name was still on the list. The exhilaration swelled up inside me. This little column in the newspaper represented the first time that I had truly achieved something important, against odds, and by sustained effort. I felt that now I was beginning to earn the respect of my friends and family that I so badly wanted. I wondered what Mrs. Buckner would think.

The next morning when I walked into the office, A.D. and Helen had taped the column of those passing the bar on the door. Move over, Clarence Darrow.

Sarah and I had made the acquaintance of a young couple who had moved to town from out of state, and the husband turned out to be my first client. It had to do with his will. It didn't quite rise to the level of importance of drafting a new will. He wanted me to review one that he already had. I inquired as to his present circumstances and his plans. I reviewed the documents, even absenting myself to sneak a look at a statute in the Tennessee Code. I then pronounced the document adequate and not in need of revision. I was very pleased with myself. It seemed to me a classic example of American jurisprudence being played out. The wise counselor—learned in the law and a trustworthy recipient of his client's most personal information—providing his sound judgment with regard to most important matters. Oh, the majesty of it all. I charged him $5.00.

Eager to get into court, I took a case that probably didn't

pass the main test for a lawyer to take a contingency fee case to court—the probability of success. If I didn't win, I wouldn't get paid. My client—a young man whose last name was Wisdom—pulled his car onto Highway 43 running out of Lawrenceburg from a dirt road into the path of an oncoming large truck. I had noticed that in everyday parlance, people would often use the term "run over" when someone would get hit by a car. In my boy Wisdom's case, saying he was run over was not hyperbole. He was run over. He had tire marks across his stomach. I was flabbergasted by the fact that the boy was not dead. But as folks around town would say, "Them Wisdoms are tough." That seemed to explain it.

The unfavorable facts of the case served as no deterrent to Wisdom, who needed a payday, or to me, who needed a case. I scrounged around in the law books, and we sued the trucking company on the theory of "last clear chance," a legal doctrine that basically says that even if the plaintiff (Wisdom) is negligent, if the defendant had an opportunity to avoid the accident or had the last clear chance to do so, then the defendant can be held liable, unless the plaintiff had engaged in willful or wanton misconduct. So I argued to the jury that even if Wisdom had been negligent in pulling out in front of the truck, he was not guilty of willful or wanton conduct and the truck had time to avoid Wisdom's automobile easily.

On the other side, representing the trucking company's

insurer, was a young lawyer from Columbia, Tennessee, named Charles Trost, who was not a lot older than I was. Charlie now practices law in Nashville and has remained a good friend over the years. Anyway, Charlie and I went round for round arguing our case. The facts of the case were clear (unfortunately). Therefore, it seemed that my oratorical skills were going to have to carry the day—so when I was arguing to the jury, long after it had become time for me to sit down, I felt this tug on my coat as I walked by counsel's table. A.D. was trying to suggest surreptitiously to me that when you are in a hole it is best to stop digging. Still, I kept pounding. My client was not guilty of wanton actions.

The case went to the jury, and hours later it became obvious that they were deadlocked, unable to reach a verdict. Finally, Judge Ingram declared that we had a hung jury. It meant that we would have to try it again.

The jury was dismissed, and as I was gathering my papers at counsel's table, one of the old fellows who was on the jury walked over to me and said, "Fred, I just want you to know I stuck with you. I think you were absolutely right. The boy was not 'wantin'' to get hurt."

I didn't know whether to laugh or cry. The old guy was in the right church but in the wrong pew. I thought about this fellow many times over the years. Whether in law or politics, it's not so much what you are saying that's important. What's important is what is being heard. Also, the more I thought about it, the more it occurred to me that this old farmer's thinking was not that far off from what the writers of that statute meant.

Sarah and I settled into the pleasant predictabilities of small-town Southern life where we had both been raised, where three generations of our family now lived. It was also where every street, park, or building brought back memories (and sometimes cringes) of games, jobs, fistfights, dates, and the first time for almost everything. We lived in a little house on the edge of town about ten minutes from the office, church, and the Little League baseball field. For the little guys, we had a minor league in which Tony played and I coached.

Sarah taught high school in Summertown, a sixteen-mile commute. It was even a smaller and a more country town than Lawrenceburg, and Sarah would come home with tales of kids talking about Sunday dinner of possum and chocolate gravy.

Law practice was the standard small-town fare of wills and estates (if you use the word estates loosely), property-line disputes, divorces, drunk-driving charges, and an occasional serious crime. Every morning, the lawyers would congregate in a little room in the upstairs corner of the courthouse that served as the general sessions courtroom, where we argued over misdemeanors, small claims, and who got to the intersection first, and to see what the Highway Patrol catch had been the night before.

Monday morning was what we called the "couple of beers docket." The Highway Patrol would parade the DWI offenders in one at a time and, whether the plea was guilty or not guilty or whether they were knee-walking drunk, most of them had had the proverbial "couple of beers." The idea, of course, was that the defendant would be more credible if he acknowledged lack of perfection in his defense of the outrageous claim that he was drunk as a skunk.

After court, four or five of the regulars would congregate at Beckham's Drug Store to drink coffee, laugh about one another's clients, talk politics, and negotiate cases.

Not too long after we tried the Wisdom case, Charlie called me up and we settled, avoiding another trial. He had talked his insurance company into offering a modest but satisfactory amount, as I recall. I never was sure whether Charlie pushed to settle the case because he didn't want to go through another one of my final arguments or because he didn't want to risk the uncertainties presented by a Lawrence County jury.

The best thing that came out of the Wisdom case was a little conversation that the circuit judge who tried the case, Judge Ingram, had with my dad. Judge Ingram had been on the bench since Moses was in rushes. He still rode the circuit like they did in the old days on a horse. His circuit covered four or five counties, and he went from county to county trying up the backlog of cases. It was an elective office, and the judge had to be a pretty good politician, at least to get elected the first time. He knew my dad, who had attended every day of my first trial with great pride and to point out any mistakes I might make. Judge Ingram called Fletch over after the trial and told him, "He did better than any young lawyer I have ever seen." Of course, Dad and I took what this old politician was telling him at total face value.

When I started practicing, I developed a solid friendship with Jim Weatherford, who was the youngest member of the leading firm in town, which did most of the personal-injury work. That, of course, is the area of the law where the money is. Insurance companies can pay more than farmers. Jim later became a circuit judge himself.

Jim was a few years older than I was, with a dry but reliable sense of humor. He was a slow-talking, slow-moving country lawyer with a sharp intellect. He sort of took me under his wing as I tried to learn the practicalities of making a living as a country lawyer. Jim provided me with one of my most creative opportunities during my first couple of years of law practice. One that had nothing to do with legal talent.

One day I received in the mail a copy of a letter that Jim had obviously written to his client—a fellow by the name of F. D. Thompson. Even though the address didn't match, these were my initials and the letter had been delivered to me. Jim had written to an insurance company on behalf of his client, Mr. Thompson, making certain claims about his client's virtues and saying that the insurance company should pay him a certain amount because of the egregious wrongs that they had visited upon him. Jim, of course, had thought he'd sent a copy of this letter to his client; instead, it was accidentally sent to me.

I thought for a minute and felt a broad smile cross my face. Across the bottom of the copy I wrote, "This is the lousiest excuse for a letter I have ever read. You're fired." And I signed it F. D. Thompson. I mailed it back to Jim in an unmarked envelope. Well, needless to say, this led to ramifications. I learned later that Jim demanded that his client come into the office, and when he did he presented the fellow with the copy of the letter that Jim thought the client had sent. Jim asked, "I just want to know what is wrong with this letter." Of course, the startled and baffled Mr. Thompson knew nothing about the letter or the copy or the handwriting on the bottom of the copy. After he had protested his innocence enough to calm Jim down, Jim demanded, "Well, who would have done something like this?" Mr. Thompson replied, "Must have been them fellows who started this whole thing in the first place."

A few days later, I called Jim to tell him what I had done, and he brought me up to date with regard to what had transpired, what he had thought, his conversation with his client, Mr. Thompson, and what he thought about me as I practically rolled on the ground with laughter. From then on, when I called Jim I would tell his secretary it was Mr. F. D. Thompson calling. And he would pick up the phone and cuss me again. Our friendship never skipped a beat, but I watched my back for a while. If a lawyer did something like that today, he would probably be called up before fourteen different bar committees and be sued by the other lawyer's client.

We continued to share the lighter moments of the country practice. I represented the man and Jim represented the woman in a divorce proceeding. The man came in and said to me, "The Mrs. and I have already worked out a settlement. We are going to sell the farm and divide it up. I am going to get the pigs, Johnny, Suzie, and the fruit jars, and wife is going to get the furniture, the goats, Mary, and Tommy." In other words, they were dividing the kids up right along with the furniture and the livestock.

Every good lawyer learns when to cut his losses—when his hard work, skills, and eloquence are clearly overmatched. The community of Loretto lies south of Lawrenceburg and close to the Alabama line. Loretto is known for a few different things, in addition to being the home of David Weathers, longtime major-league baseball pitcher who is relieving currently for the Milwaukee Brewers. One is casket manufacturing. For some reason, it has become the home of several such plants over the years.

The owner of one of those plants came to me with a story

that has to be every casket manufacturer's nightmare. You guessed it. As the dearly and recently departed was being carried down the church center aisle, the bottom fell out of you know what. The lawsuits were being filed almost as soon as the body hit the floor. The casket was purchased at a funeral home, and the books were in such bad shape that it was not certain who manufactured the casket. Although my client, the casket manufacturer, was being sued, he didn't really think that it was his casket. It had to do with the number of screws placed in the bottom of the casket. As a matter of practice, my client placed more screws in the bottom than the casket in question contained.

The funeral home bought caskets from my client as well as other manufacturers. It seemed to me that this was a pretty defendable case. The burden of proof was on the plaintiff, who would have to prove that our factory produced the offending casket. Unfortunately, my battle plan failed to survive its first encounter with the enemy. As I watched the plaintiff's counsel give his opening statement and describe what had happened in the church that day, the thud of the floor, the reaction of the mourners, and the dress (or undress) of the corpse, it seemed to me that at least two or three of the female jurors were on the verge of fainting. I got the distinct impression that the jurors who were not overcome with revulsion were at least thinking about their own loved ones. When I got up to explain my missing screw theory, half of them were looking at the ceiling and the other half were peering at me through squinted eyes. It reminded me that we were trying the case in the hometown of the deceased. Being a young man of great sensitivity and acute perception, I decided that this was not a good situation (something I should have decided about six months earlier). I asked for a continuance. We settled the case, and I got out of town as quickly as possible. Maybe I should have told them we weren't "wantin'" to hurt nobody.

Soon after we moved back to Lawrenceburg, I informed my folks and the Lindseys that I had thrown in with the Republicans, and I received no pushback. I had the feeling that if they had been my age, they would have done the same thing.

The more I watched the national scene and what I felt to be the liberal drift of the Democratic Party, and the more I immersed myself into conservative thought—I grabbed whatever it was William F. Buckley was writing at the time—the more I realized that the Republican Party was going to be the place for me. If I had had personal political ambition, I might have thought longer about it, because Tennessee was definitely a Democratic state, from the local, Lawrence County level up to the statehouse and the governor's mansion. The Democrats held both United States Senate seats and five of the seven congressional seats. In 1964, home from college, I briefly shook the hand of a young lawyer from East Tennessee by the name of Howard Baker, Jr. He was trying to become the first popularly elected Republican for the Senate since the Civil War. However, he was running in a year that would not be good for Republicans nationally. In addition to the general political trend that year, Senator Barry Goldwater's coming to Tennessee and suggesting that the TVA be sold did not prove to be extremely beneficial to Baker's chances. He lost that election, but he came back two years later, in 1966, and won. The chance meeting we had at the courthouse in Lawrenceburg, as he was campaigning, was the beginning of a political and personal friendship that would have a great influence on my life. In 1973 he brought me to Washington to be the Watergate Committee's Republican counsel. More than forty years after our first meeting, we would be standing almost on the same spot on the square as he introduced me at a rally during my run for the Republican presidential nomination.

Although I had no desire and I was in no position to run for political office, I was recruited to run for the state legislature by the Republican leader in the Tennessee state house, Hal Carter. He was the brother of Dixie Carter, of *Designing Women* fame. From Hal Carter's visits I learned that what they say is true about what happens when a couple of people suggest that you run for office: You tend to consider that a groundswell of public support. I was indeed tempted, though my heavily Democratic district dissuaded me.

However, in 1968 I was approached about becoming the campaign manager for a fellow by the name of John T. Williams, who was running against the entrenched congressman of our district, Ray Blanton. As I indicated earlier, Blanton would prove to be another political figure whose path I would cross more than once. I was excited and honored that the powers that be of the Republican establishment in our district (both of them) thought I could do this job. Although I knew how uphill the battle would be, I had no idea how hopeless the endeavor was. The fact that they were turning to a kid just out of school to manage a congressional campaign should have been my first clue. John T. was a very nice, energetic fellow in his mid-fifties who'd served as a United States marshal. He was determined to shake every hand in the district and do his dead level best to win.

Despite the odds, there were other issues that might have given a saner man pause. The campaign headquarters, where I would have to spend the majority of my time, was in Jackson, Tennessee, about seventy miles away. The campaign had no money at that time and I would have to sleep in the campaign headquarters. So if I took on this task, it would mean living out of a suitcase, sleeping on a couch, with low pay for a hopeless cause. Naturally, with Sarah's blessing, I took the job.

I spent most of my days and many of my nights on the telephone trying to raise money, scheduling the candidate, putting out fires among local bickering supporters, and filling in as a surrogate for the candidate. We finally raised enough money to put up some billboards. I decided that our theme should be "John T. Williams. To help clean up the mess in Washington." Sound familiar? The theme may have been pretty effective, but we never got to find out. The billboards, as it turned out, were so far back off the highway, and the "To help clean up the mess in Washington" part was printed in such small letters, that you couldn't read the words from the road.

There was one event in that campaign that was especially significant for me. Governor Ronald Reagan of California was barnstorming for several Republican candidates across the country and made a speech for my candidate at the Coliseum in Jackson, Tennessee. As campaign manager I got to sit backstage with Governor Reagan for a few minutes before he went onstage. He turned to me and said, "What do you think I ought to tell them?" Taken by surprise, I gave him a few thoughts. I said, "I'd just acknowledge that you don't know John T. personally but that you know what he stands for. And it's the same thing that you stand for." He went out and said exactly what I had suggested. So Reagan had me for life even before I really understood his philosophy. His philosophy was a bonus.

John T. was the most energetic campaigner I'd met, but on election night I learned one of those lessons that has to be experienced firsthand before it hits home: Don't expect to win a race against a popular incumbent congressman when you have very little money. We lost every county in the district except one. I was encouraged by the fact that we almost carried Lawrence County.

I resumed my law practice, exhilarated by the experience but glad to get back to my profession, where results were at least somewhat related to effort. However, in 1968 something else occurred that would have a major impact on my career—the election of Richard Nixon as president. It seemed like a very faraway event and something that had nothing to do with me. Actually, the presidential election had been a watershed election for Tennessee and the South. People were becoming more and more concerned about the breakdown in law and order and civil society that we were increasingly seeing on our TV screens. These sentiments were held by many Tennessee Democrats who voted for Nixon, allowing him to carry the state.

As the joke goes about drug users, "If you remember the 1960s, you weren't there." I was one of the ones who wasn't there. As things were heating up, I was settling down. Ironically, I had missed the countercultural rebellion that was being carried out in the streets, but in a way I became a beneficiary of it.

In 1968 a new president appointed not only all of the United States Attorneys but all of the Assistant United States Attorneys, as well. My name came up in political circles as a possible AUSA in Nashville. I was also helped by the fact that there were precious few young Republican lawyers in

Middle Tennessee at that time. Early in 1969, I received an offer from the newly appointed U.S. Attorney, Charles Anderson, to become one of his five assistants in Nashville. The office had jurisdiction over forty counties in Middle Tennessee, including Lawrence County. The offer was somewhat unexpected and exciting. It had never really occurred to me that I would leave Lawrenceburg, and I received advice from some of the leading attorneys there that moving to Nashville at this stage of my career would be a mistake. I was just establishing myself, getting to know the judges and starting to develop a reputation. All of that would be set back if I went to Nashville. However, by taking the job of Assistant United States Attorney, I would be one of the higher-ranking federal legal figures in Middle Tennessee, trying federal criminal and civil cases. This was no small potatoes for a fellow who had just been out of law school for two years. Sarah and I discussed this extensively, and, as usual, we had a meeting of the minds that this looked like an adventure too interesting to pass up. However, I told A.D. of my decision with very mixed emotions and not at all sure that I was doing the right thing. He seemed to understand. Besides, I planned to get the experience and return to Lawrenceburg in a couple of years, because at heart I was a country lawyer. Of course, we never moved back, even though that "heart" part has never changed.

Upon arriving in Nashville, I learned that I had about as

much trial experience as anyone else in that office, and before long I was prosecuting most of the serious federal crime cases. I proudly displayed my certificate of appointment on my office wall. It was signed by Attorney General John Mitchell. The first time I met John Mitchell, however, was when I was interrogating him three years later in the middle of the Watergate investigation.

A Good Man

PROBABLY LIKE MOST PEOPLE of my generation and younger, I am amazed at how ubiquitous smoking is in the old classic movies. It was the epitome of cool. When I watch oldies, I marvel at the old-time moviemakers' ability to keep continuity with regard to the length of the cigarette the actor is smoking when a simple scene might be shot over a time span of hours or even days. This is part of the cost of knowing the inside of moviemaking—noticing the triviali-ties when trying to relax and enjoy the movie. Smart-aleck movie watchers (myself excepted, of course) and movie re-viewers like nothing better than to point out that the blinds were pulled in the first part of the scene and open in the last part without anyone on-screen having opened them.

I had to deal with the cigarette continuity problem only once in a movie. Although I never smoked cigarettes, I smoked through a scene with Alec Baldwin. (There's no truth to the rumor that his political views drove me to it. To drink, maybe, but not to smoke.) We were doing a scene in *Hunt for Red October* in which I played an admiral. I had no trouble adapting. I smoked that cigarette and held it just the way that Dad always did. It was a bittersweet remembrance.

By the time people became aware of the harmful effects of smoking, Dad had long since become addicted. Finally, after many years, common sense won out and he quit—cold turkey. Apparently, the decision had come too late.

In 1990, when my parents were on a trip to Arizona, Dad felt a pain in his chest. He had a pretty good idea as to what the problem was. For most of his life he was a two- or three-pack-a-day man. He started out by rolling his own out of store-bought cigarette paper and a pouch of Country Gentleman tobacco.

When the pain became severe, they turned the car around and headed home. In a remarkable feat of stamina, Dad drove straight through from Arizona to Lawrenceburg. He wanted to know, and the diagnosis was quick to follow. It was as bad as feared. When Mom told me that Dad had lung cancer, there was a feeling of unreality about it all. For a while I had trouble imagining something that Dad couldn't handle. But over the next several months he steadily declined.

It was the most remarkable thing. Nothing about him changed. He was dying the way he lived—a little melancholy, and trying not to take things any more seriously than absolutely necessary.

During his many days in the hospital, he struck up a friendship with one particular nurse—a portly black lady whose wit was a fair match for Dad's. One day something came up about smoking. She said to Dad, "You know, I'm a nurse and I smoked for ten years before I could give it up."

Dad thought for a minute and said, "Well, I smoked heavy for about fifty years." He paused and then said with a straight face, "And I was just getting good at it."

She just smiled, shook her head, and walked out of the room. She thought she was going to have a serious conversation about smoking, but there would be no mea culpas from Fletcher—not to any of us mortals, anyway.

The decision was made to operate and remove part of one of Dad's lungs—a substantial part, as it turned out. Immediately after the operation, they rolled him to where I and other family members were. He was barely conscious and had tubes running from everywhere. I walked beside the gurney with the doctor, a nurse, and others on the way to intensive care. As our somber procession made its way down the hall, Dad motioned to me. I could tell he wanted to write something. I gave him a pen and a scrap of paper that I had on me. With a weak and shaky hand he wrote the word *SUE* and handed it back to his lawyer son. To the dismay of all around me, I doubled over in laughter. And for some reason, when I showed it to the surgeon, he didn't seem to think it was as funny as I did.

Four months later, Dad passed away. For all those months in the hospital, Mom spent every night with him in his room, with rare exceptions. Later, she moved to Franklin, Tennessee, in the Nashville area where my brother Ken and I lived.

It was sort of the Thompson male tradition not to share much of a personal nature about our feelings with one another. I guess we never felt the need to. I knew all I needed to know about Dad, from the lessons he taught me, but mostly by the way he lived his life. I heard Senator Sam Irvin of Watergate fame say something that stayed with me: "If you can paint a really good picture of a cow, you don't have to write the word 'cow' under it." To me, Dad had painted a really good picture of a cow. Yet there is another dimension to a person that often comes out on their best and worst days. Dad had suffered through some awful days, but he had the calm and inner strength of the proverbial Christian holding four aces, which is how he viewed himself.

It may seem odd to revisit such a sad and painful time and emphasize the humorous things he said and did, but those are some of the things that made him the unique man that he was. When life's absurd happenings and ironies presented themselves and seemed to require us to either laugh or cry, Fletch always chose to laugh if at all possible—or better still, make someone else laugh. It was never calculated; he never told jokes as such. His take on things was immediate and honest.

A Good Man

Amid the sadness that his humor helped mask, he knew at the end that he had been a good man and done his best. Just because a man isn't famous or doesn't leave a lot of money doesn't mean he doesn't leave a legacy. A part of Dad's is the fact that, all these years later, I often still experience situations that cause me to think, "What would Dad say about that?" And I smile.

It was January 28, 1995. I was sitting at my desk on the floor of the United States Senate prior to delivering my maiden speech. It was in support of a bill I was cosponsoring that required members of Congress in the operation of their offices to abide by the same laws that other citizens had to follow (a revolutionary concept even then). I figured that if members of Congress had to abide by the employment, OSHA, and other laws that they imposed upon American businesses and citizens, they would be more careful in the passage of such laws. I had been sworn in a few days earlier. Someone on behalf of the leadership was droning on to an almost empty chamber about the agenda for the day. I assumed that the speaker was stalling long enough for the crowd to assemble to hear my speech. Even the section for the press corps was empty. Perhaps they had heard me speak before.

As I gazed around the beautiful and historic surroundings, my eyes fell on the gallery above me and to my right.

That's where I had sat by myself one afternoon twenty-seven years earlier, a year out of law school. I'd come to Washington for the Young Republicans Convention at the Shoreham Hotel, but having grown weary of the organized activities there, I snuck away to watch Senators Goldwater, Humphrey, and other political giants of the day deliberate the issues. I'd been transfixed. Now instead of observing, I was participating.

For me, the trip from the Senate gallery to the Senate floor had been a long one. I was pleased about the way things had worked out. I had been given a rare opportunity to make a difference in the direction of my country. A couple of years earlier, I had made the decision to leave a life that would have been the envy of a lot of people to win an uphill Senate campaign, and this speech was going to be the beginning of my opportunity to make a difference.

As I got into the speech I worked in American history, the Constitution, the common sense of the American people, and why the Senate could not afford to turn its back on this important piece of legislation. I thought I was laying the groundwork for a new era of responsibility in Washington.

As I was gathering my papers together after the speech, one of the few senators still on the floor, an older gentleman, came over to me, extended his hands in congratulations, and said, "Good speech, Fred." It was a moment of great personal satisfaction. Then he said, "Can I ask you just one question?"

"Absolutely," I responded, prepared to defend my position. He said, "Was that a real submarine that you fellows used in *Hunt for Red October*?"

There was only one fellow I knew who could have fully appreciated that story. I wish I could have told it to him.

On Being Lucky

I GREW UP at a time when the United States was starting to reach its full potential. We were becoming the most powerful and economically successful country in the history of the world and were beginning to make real strides toward social justice. We became the symbol for freedom around the world.

After World War II, people came off the farm and into small towns all over the South, bringing with them their independence, strong religious beliefs, and often a humorous take on life that probably helped them deal with the hard times so many of them endured.

There was an underlying sense of optimism tempered by fatalism: "You can't control the weather. There'll be a better crop next year." There were absolutes. Your word was your bond. A lot depended on it if they were going to build a civil society. There was an understanding that their life was better than their parents' and a strong belief that their kids' life would be better than their own. I really don't believe that my parents' generation thought that they "could be anything they wanted to be." Theirs was a generation that just wanted life to be a little better than it had been. But they inculcated into the next generation—my generation—a firm belief that *we* could be anything we wanted to be. That belief, assumption really, has been the basis for any success I have had.

Growing up in Lawrenceburg, I was taught that I was supposed to handle the things that I had control over and deal with the rest "like a man."

But I have wondered, How much do we have control over, anyway? Some people believe that everything has been predetermined by the Man upstairs. Others believe that we are all on our own. I have come down somewhere in the middle.

Many of us feel a bit like the farmer who labored long and hard to clear what folks back home called "a new ground." He sweated and toiled until he and his mule were exhausted and every stump was removed from the field. As he looked it over one day, the preacher pulled up and said, "My, my, the Lord sure has blessed you with a beautiful farm."

Trying to hide his irritation, the farmer replied, "Yes, he

really did. But you should have seen it when he had it all to himself."

Life is a partnership. Part of it is up to Him and part of it is up to us. But unlike the farmer, we can never be certain which part is which.

I appreciate the interrelatedness of the choices I have made on the one hand, and luck on the other. Life presents us with a series of doors. Some are locked, some are wide open, and some are open just a bit—just enough to reveal some intriguing shadows behind them. But not quite enough to reveal exactly what that something is. Is it something wonderful or something treacherous? Is opportunity waiting or is sadness lurking? We will never know if we don't walk through the door. Should we play it safe? There is a lot to be said for playing it safe. But safe is not very interesting. At least, I never found it to be. And it's a lot better if we can make our decisions with a sense of confidence and optimism that comes from seeds planted in our early years.

Then there's the luck part. I often tell aspiring candidates, half in jest, that the most brilliant politicians are the ones whose daddy left them a fortune or who run for office in a year when their party is sweeping everything. In other words, the key is to be the beneficiary of things totally out of their control. But, of course, there's more to luck than that.

Being *really* lucky is being born in the United States to

good parents. The acorn still doesn't fall far from the tree. Our parents, the community we grew up in, and our early experiences form the core of our character, affect the decisions that we make and the course of our lives. I know this better than most.

Even before I left Lawrenceburg, you might say I was given a second chance more than once. Every difficult kid who has grown out of it has a different story to tell. Instead of searching for any commonality between these kids, it's probably more important to just realize that it does happen. It happens quite often. Understanding this has caused me to view kids who have underachieved, or who seemed less focused, quite differently than I otherwise might. More than once I've smiled and said to myself, "There goes another Freddie Thompson. I hope he is as lucky as I was." My mistakes in life would fill another book, but I've been able to have multiple careers, none of which were thought remotely possible for me when I walked across the stage at high school graduation.

Who knows what provides the wake-up call for a kid. I believe that potential has to be inside a person to begin with in order to be brought out, but it is often found in the most unlikely young people. We should not give up on these kids. Meeting the right people, being tested by some hard times, receiving encouragement, and having a little luck can make all the difference in the world. Sometimes even that streak of rebellion and hardheadedness can mask a sense of individualism and adventuresomeness that can serve a person well and take them to some very interesting places. Don't be too hard on the rebel without a clue. Maybe the less he does today, the more he's going to do tomorrow.

Acknowledgments

I want to express my appreciation to Sean Desmond of Crown Publishers for having the concept for this book and believing that my stories about growing up in a small town would bring a smile and a warm feeling to a lot of folks. Also, thanks to my agent, Mel Berger, for his steadfast friendship and guidance.

In writing this book, I relied upon friends who so often have been there for me before, including Ed McFadden. He gave me wise counsel in shaping and editing the manuscript. Here I also include Alex Castellanos, whose insights and ideas have always served me well. A special thanks to Bobbie Murphy, my assistant for many years, who did everything from research and typing manuscripts to serving as my "humor meter" while she read my stories.

I am deeply indebted to Sarah Knestrick; to my children, Tony, Betsy, and Daniel; to the people I grew up with in Lawrenceburg; and especially to Mom, Dad, and Ken, all of whom created the bittersweet memories I write about and inspired a small-town boy to reach beyond his grasp.

Acknowledgments

Finally, I want to express my love and gratitude to my wife, Jeri, who not only served as my best sounding board, but helped and encouraged me in this endeavor. It is a trip I could not have made without her.

Index

Index

Index

Index